THE MINI FARMING AND SELF-SUFFICIENCY BIBLE

[4 IN 1] CRAFTING A SUSTAINABLE FUTURE
THROUGH THOUGHTFUL PLANNING, CULTIVATING HARVESTS,
NURTURING SMALL LIVESTOCK,
AND HARNESSING RENEWABLE ENERGIES

ETHAN J. MITCHELL

TABLE OF CONTENTS

INTRODUCTION

Agriculture has, for millennia, stood as the linchpin of human societies, continuously evolving in response to the needs of populations and environmental challenges. Over the years, various agricultural methodologies have been developed and adopted, each with its own merits and limitations. Within this backdrop, Mini Farming emerges as a modern, sustainable, and high-efficiency practice, particularly suited for urban and peri-urban settings. This introduction aims to outline the concept of Mini Farming, provide an overview of intensive agriculture, discuss how Mini Farming can be implemented in diverse settings, and underline the increasingly critical importance of self-sufficiency in the contemporary world.

Mini Farming, as the name suggests, involves the practice of agriculture on a reduced scale. However, it isn't about merely scaling down traditional agricultural practices; rather, Mini Farming focuses on resource optimization and efficient space utilization. The primary goal is to maximize yield per unit area, while simultaneously reducing environmental impact. This might include, but isn't limited to, techniques such as vertical farming, the use of organic compost, introducing drip irrigation systems, and adopting no-till farming methods. The end result is an agricultural system capable of producing a significant amount of food in a confined area, often with reduced inputs and minimal environmental impact.

Intensive agriculture, often seen as the antithesis of Mini Farming, represents the prevailing trend in modern agricultural industry. This form of agriculture focuses on the mass production of food through intense resource usage, maximizing every inch of available land.

This involves the use of large machinery, dependence on chemical pesticides and fertilizers, and adopting practices aimed at maximizing short-term yields. While intensive agriculture has the merit of producing vast quantities of food, this often comes at the cost of the environment. Issues such as soil erosion, reduced biodiversity, water contamination, and greenhouse gas emissions are all direct or indirect consequences of this form of agriculture.

Mini Farming is not a "one-size-fits-all" solution, but rather a set of principles and practices that can be adapted to various contexts. Whether it's an urban garden, a peri-urban plot of land, or a small rural community, Mini Farming techniques can be applied to achieve optimal results. For instance, in an urban setting, the use of vertical gardens and adopting container farming techniques can allow for a surprisingly diverse range of plants to be cultivated in constrained spaces. Similarly, in a rural setting, crop rotation, polyculture, and utilizing local resources can improve soil health and increase yields.

In an age of globalization and interdependence, the ability to produce food locally becomes increasingly significant. Fluctuations in the global market, disruptions in supply chains, and growing environmental concerns make self-sufficiency not only desirable but often essential. Mini Farming, with its emphasis on local and sustainable production, offers a solution to these challenges. It not only reduces dependence on imports and minimizes environmental impact but also promotes community resilience, biodiversity conservation, and safeguards soil health.

In summary, while intensive agriculture has dominated the farming landscape for decades, new approaches like Mini Farming are emerging as high-efficiency, sustainable alternatives. In a world where resources are finite and sustainability is paramount, the ability to produce food efficiently and environmentally-consciously becomes paramount. Through the adoption of Mini Farming principles and promoting self-sufficiency, we can move towards an agricultural model that not only feeds populations but also protects and enhances our precious environment.

BOOK 1

CHAPTER 1

HISTORY OF MINI FARMING

FROM AGRICULTURAL ORIGINS TO THE INDUSTRIAL REVOLUTION

THE DAWN OF AGRICULTURE

The history of agriculture traces back approximately 10,000 years. Early humans transitioned from nomadic hunting and gathering to settled agriculture. These ancient agricultural systems were fundamentally 'mini' by today's standards. Small plots of cultivated land yielded crops that sustained small familial units and, eventually, larger communities.

Crop Domestication: The earliest agricultural societies chose plants with desirable traits and selectively cultivated them over generations. This selective farming led to the domestication of many crops we recognize today, like wheat, rice, and maize.

Tools and Techniques: The Neolithic agriculturalists employed rudimentary tools made of stone, wood, and bone. They practiced basic farming methods like slash-and-burn, wherein forests were cleared, burned, and replaced with crops.

ANCIENT CIVILIZATIONS AND THEIR AGRICULTURAL INNOVATIONS

Mesopotamia: Often dubbed the 'Cradle of Civilization,' Mesopotamia saw the cultivation of barley, emmer, and dates. The Sumerians invented the plow, improving tilling efficiency.

Ancient Egypt: The Nile's annual flood enriched the riverbanks, creating a fertile stretch. This allowed for the intensive cultivation of wheat and barley. Hieroglyphs also depict small garden plots, indicating the presence of mini farming.

Ancient China: The fertile plains of the Yellow River saw the cultivation of millet and rice. Terrace farming, a mini farming precursor, was practiced in hilly regions.

The Americas: Before European contact, Native Americans practiced the 'Three Sisters' farming method, growing maize, beans, and squash together in small plots, exemplifying early mini farming techniques.

THE MEDIEVAL ERA

The Middle Ages experienced significant agricultural advancements. Manorial systems dominated Europe, where lords owned vast lands, and peasants worked on them. Despite the scale, many peasants maintained their own small gardens for subsistence.

Crop Rotation: This era saw the rise of the three-field system, rotating between grains, legumes, and fallow periods to prevent soil exhaustion.

Technological Advancements: The heavy plow, horse collar, and watermills improved efficiency, allowing for more intensive farming.

THE INDUSTRIAL REVOLUTION: A TURNING POINT

The Industrial Revolution in the 18th and 19th centuries was a significant turning point. Urbanization accelerated as people moved to cities for work, reducing the agricultural workforce.

Agricultural Mechanization: Innovations like the seed drill, mechanical reaper, and threshing machine revolutionized farming practices, favoring large-scale farms over smaller plots.

Enclosure Movement: In places like Britain, common lands were enclosed, consolidating fields and promoting large-scale farming. This led to a decline in small-scale or 'mini' farming.

Transportation: Railways and better road networks allowed for the transport of agricultural goods over long distances, reducing the need for local, smaller farms in proximity to urban centers.

RETURNING TO THE ROOTS: THE RENAISSANCE OF MINI FARMING

THE 20TH CENTURY: CHANGES ON THE HORIZON

Post the two World Wars, there was a significant push towards industrial farming, backed by technological advancements and a growing global population. However, by the late 20th century, concerns over sustainability, health, and local produce began emerging.

Green Revolution: While it increased food production exponentially through high-yielding varieties and synthetic fertilizers, the Green Revolution also brought concerns about biodiversity loss, environmental damage, and the marginalization of small-scale farmers.

MINI FARMING: A MODERN RESPONSE

As the 21st century dawned, a conscious shift towards sustainable, organic, and local produce began taking center stage, giving impetus to the renaissance of mini farming.

Urban Agriculture: With limited space in urban areas, rooftops, balconies, and small plots became centers for mini farming, producing fresh vegetables and herbs.

Community Gardens: These shared spaces became popular, especially in urban settings, allowing communities to come together to cultivate produce.

Permaculture: This holistic approach to agriculture emphasized sustainable and self-sufficient practices, often executed on smaller plots, resonating with mini farming principles.

Technological Advancements: Modern technology has also played a role in this resurgence. Drip irrigation, vertical farming, and hydroponics have made it feasible to farm intensively in small spaces.

ECONOMIC AND ENVIRONMENTAL FACTORS

Local and Organic Demand: With increased awareness about food sources and environmental impacts, there's been a surge in demand for local and organic produce, which mini farms are well-positioned to provide.

Biodiversity and Soil Health: Mini farms, with their diverse crops and organic practices, play a crucial role in maintaining biodiversity and promoting soil health, acting as a counter to large-scale monocultures.

Economic Empowerment: Mini farming provides avenues for entrepreneurship and self-sufficiency, especially in urban and peri-urban settings.

In tracing the history of mini farming, it's evident that the practice has come full circle. From its origins in the early days of agriculture to its decline during the Industrial Revolution and subsequent revival in the modern era, mini farming remains an integral aspect of the human relationship with the land. It underscores the constant endeavor to balance growth with sustainability, innovation with tradition, and global perspectives with local imperatives.

CHAPTER 2

PLANNING AND DESIGNING YOUR MINI FARM

RAISED BEDS

UNDERSTANDING THE CONCEPT OF RAISED BEDS

A raised bed is a garden bed that sits above the natural ground level. These beds are typically confined using some material – be it wood, stone, metal, or even composite materials. Their popularity has surged, particularly in urban settings, but their benefits make them a viable choice for any agricultural enthusiast, regardless of the location.

THE MULTIFACETED BENEFITS OF RAISED BEDS

Soil Quality Control: One of the foremost advantages of raised beds is the ability to control soil composition. Gardeners can use specialized mixes tailored to their crops, ensuring that plants get the best medium for their growth.

Improved Drainage: Due to their elevation, raised beds generally offer superior drainage. This can be a lifesaver, particularly in regions prone to heavy rainfall. Better drainage means less water stagnation, reducing the risk of root rot and other moisture-related complications.

Fewer Soil Compaction Issues: Traditional in-ground gardens often suffer from soil compaction, which can hinder plant roots' growth. Raised beds, due to their defined space and reduced foot traffic, typically face fewer such issues.

Pest Management: Raised beds can act as a barrier to several ground pests, such as slugs, snails, and certain soil-borne diseases. Additionally, the height can make it harder for pests to reach plants, although it's not a foolproof solution.

Ergonomics: The elevation means reduced bending and stooping, a boon for those with back problems or mobility issues. Gardening becomes more accessible and enjoyable, catering to a wider range of physical abilities.

ESSENTIAL CONSIDERATIONS IN DESIGNING RAISED BEDS

Material Choices: The material used for bed boundaries can influence aesthetics, durability, and even plant health. For instance, cedar and redwood are rot-resistant and can last several years. Stone or brick offers permanence and a rustic charm. However, treated wood can potentially leach chemicals into the soil and is best avoided.

Ideal Dimensions: While length and width are often dictated by available space, depth is crucial. A depth of 6-8 inches might suffice for shallow-rooted crops, but for deeper-rooted plants or root vegetables, 12 inches or more is recommended.

Optimal Placement: Beds should be oriented to maximize sunlight exposure. Generally, north-south orientation is preferred in many regions to ensure even sunlight distribution. However, site-specific factors such as shadows from nearby structures can affect this decision.

Spacing Between Beds: Allow sufficient room between beds for easy navigation, tool operation, and airflow. A minimum of 2-3 feet is generally advisable.

SOIL COMPOSITION AND MAINTENANCE IN RAISED BEDS

Selecting the Right Soil Mix: Starting with a blend of topsoil, compost, and coarse sand or perlite often gives a balanced, well-draining, and fertile base. This mix provides both macro and micro-nutrients, essential for plant health.

Maintaining Soil Fertility: Over time, soil nutrients get depleted. Regularly adding compost or well-decomposed manure can replenish these nutrients. Crop rotation, even within the confined space of raised beds, can also prevent nutrient exhaustion and disease build-up.

Monitoring Soil pH: The pH level, indicating soil's acidity or alkalinity, impacts nutrient availability. Most vegetables prefer slightly acidic to neutral pH (6.0-7.5). Lime can be added to raise pH (make soil more alkaline), while sulfur or peat moss can lower pH (increase acidity).

WATER MANAGEMENT IN RAISED BEDS

Efficient Watering Systems: Drip irrigation or soaker hoses ensure consistent moisture while minimizing water wastage. Overhead watering systems, while feasible, can increase disease susceptibility due to wet foliage.

Monitoring Moisture Levels: The elevated nature and improved drainage mean raised beds can dry out faster than in-ground gardens. A regular check, about an inch below the soil surface, can provide insights into watering needs.

Mulching: A layer of organic mulch, such as straw or wood chips, can help retain moisture, suppress weeds, and regulate soil temperature. It's a simple addition with multifaceted benefits.

SEASONAL CONSIDERATIONS AND CROP ROTATION

Extended Growing Season: The soil in raised beds tends to warm up faster in spring. This means an earlier start to the planting season. Conversely, in fall, these beds can retain warmth a bit longer.

Crop Rotation: Even in a mini farm setting, rotating crops can prevent soil-borne diseases and pests from becoming entrenched. It also ensures different nutrients are utilized, helping maintain soil balance.

OVERCOMING CHALLENGES WITH RAISED BEDS

While raised beds offer numerous advantages, they're not without challenges. Awareness and proactive measures can help overcome these.

Soil Erosion: Over time, soil can erode, especially after heavy rains. Installing liners at the base, using coarser soil particles, and ensuring a level bed can reduce erosion risks.

Cost: Setting up raised beds can be more expensive than traditional gardens. However, the long-term benefits in yield, reduced pest issues, and improved soil management can offset these initial costs.

Raised beds represent a blend of tradition and innovation. Their design principles are rooted in age-old agricultural practices, but their adaptation to contemporary needs makes them a staple for modern farming, especially in space-constrained or urban settings. With thoughtful planning and design, raised beds can be the cornerstone of a productive mini farm, turning even small patches of land into bountiful havens.

EVALUATION OF THE SOIL AND AVAILABLE RESOURCES

THE IMPERATIVE OF SOIL EVALUATION IN MINI FARMING

In the domain of agriculture, and particularly in the setting of mini farming, soil doesn't merely serve as a medium in which plants grow; it is the lifeline, the very foundation that determines the health, yield, and quality of the crops. Delving into its composition, understanding its type, and gauging its health are paramount to shaping a successful mini farm.

APPROACHING SOIL EVALUATION: A STRUCTURED METHODOLOGY

Soil Texture and Composition Understanding the texture of the soil is essential, as it impacts aeration, drainage, and the soil's ability to retain water. Soil is categorized into three primary particles based on size: sand, silt, and clay.

- **Sand:** The largest particle in soil. Soil with a dominant sand composition boasts excellent aeration and drainage but struggles with water retention.

- **Silt:** Intermediate-sized particles. Silt-rich soil offers a balanced structure with good water retention properties.

- **Clay:** The smallest of the three particles. Clay-dominant soil can retain a high volume of water but may lack adequate drainage, leading to potential root rot.

The combination of these three particles results in various soil types: sandy, silty, clayey, and loamy (an ideal blend of all three).

Soil pH Testing The pH level of the soil speaks volumes about its acidity or alkalinity. This measure directly impacts nutrient availability for plants. Most crops flourish in slightly acidic to neutral soil (pH 6 to 7.5). Kits are available to test soil pH, but for a comprehensive analysis, sending a sample to a local agricultural extension service is recommended.

Nutrient Analysis A nutrient assay provides insights into essential elements present in the soil: nitrogen (vital for leaf growth), phosphorus (important for root and flower development), and potassium (crucial for overall plant health). Again, specialized kits can help in this evaluation, but for detailed results, professional laboratory testing is advisable.

Soil Drainage Assessment Good drainage is crucial to prevent waterlogging. A simple test involves digging a hole about a foot deep, filling it with water, and observing the drainage rate. If the water takes too long to drain, it might indicate compacted or clay-rich soil.

Organic Matter Content Organic matter, such as decomposed plants and animals, enhances soil fertility. A dark color typically indicates a high organic content. However, for a precise measure, laboratory tests might be necessary.

EVALUATING AVAILABLE RESOURCES

In mini farming, the adage 'work smarter, not harder' rings particularly true. Maximizing output from a limited space demands judicious use of available resources.

Space Utilization Space is a premium resource in mini farming. Detailed mapping and planning are crucial. Consider vertical farming, succession planting, and companion planting techniques to optimize space.

Water Source and Management Water is a lifeblood for plants. Assessing its source, quality, and delivery methods ensures plants get optimal hydration. Employ drip irrigation or soaker hoses for efficient water use.

Tools and Equipment While mini farming doesn't demand extensive machinery like large-scale farming, certain tools can make tasks more efficient. Evaluate the tools at hand and invest in essential equipment like a good-quality hoe, rake, spade, pruners, and perhaps a small tiller.

Seeds and Plant Selection Based on the soil evaluation, choose plants best suited for the existing soil or amend the soil to expand plant choices. Procure high-quality seeds and seedlings from reputable sources.

Natural and Man-made Infrastructure Consider existing structures like walls or fences that can support trellises. Evaluate natural resources like trees for potential shade or wind barriers.

Labour and Expertise Even in mini farming, tasks can be labor-intensive. If working solo, time management becomes essential. If hiring help or collaborating with community members, ensure they bring the right skills to the table.

Budget and Financial Resources Mini farming is cost-effective, but some investment is required, especially in the initial stages. Crafting a budget and sticking to it, while keeping a buffer for unforeseen expenses, ensures sustainable farming without financial strain.

In wrapping up, understanding the intricacies of one's soil and the resources at hand isn't just a step; it's the very essence of planning and designing a mini farm. The time and effort invested in these preliminary stages lay the groundwork for a thriving, productive mini farm that is not only sustainable but also rewarding in its yield and impact.

ELABORATING ON CHOOSING THE RIGHT SIZE AND LAYOUT OF CROPS FOR MINI FARMING

THE IMPERATIVE OF MAKING CALCULATED CROP SIZE AND LAYOUT CHOICES

Contextual Understanding:
Embarking on the journey of mini farming poses unique challenges. Given the constraint of limited space, precision in the design and planning phase is paramount. The choices made in relation to the dimensions and arrangement of crops directly correlate with the farm's overall productivity and efficiency. While the objectives are clear – optimal space utilization, prolific crop growth, and heightened yields – the means to achieve these goals require a deep dive into the nuances of crop dimensioning and layout planning.

DYNAMICS STEERING CROP DIMENSIONING AND DESIGN

Defining the Mini Farm's Mission

Subsistence Farming: When the goal is to feed the family and be self-reliant, it's essential to emphasize crops that provide staple nutrition and have prolonged harvesting periods, ensuring sustained food supply.

Commercial Farming: For those looking at mini farming as a business avenue, it becomes vital to gauge market demand. Opting for crops that fetch a good price and are in demand locally can bolster profitability.

Regional Variables and their Influence

Climate Compatibility: Different crops have varying climatic preferences. It's crucial to align crop choices with the prevailing weather conditions, ensuring crops are well-suited to thrive in the local climate.

Seasonal Considerations: Awareness of the local growing seasons, their duration, and characteristics can guide the selection of crops that will mature harmoniously within these temporal constraints.

The Soil Spectrum

Soil Type Matching: Soil is not universally the same. While some crops flourish in sandy terrains, others may favor more clay-based soils. Hence, understanding and matching the soil type with crop preferences is pivotal.

Periodic Soil Analysis: Beyond just the type, the soil's nutrient profile is vital. Regular soil tests can provide insights into nutrient levels, pH balances, and other factors, enabling farmers to select crops that will thrive or amend the soil accordingly.

THE SCIENCE AND ART BEHIND DECIDING CROP DIMENSIONS

Decoding Crop Spacing

Row Dynamics: The distance between rows should not just accommodate the present size of the crop but its full-grown stature. Moreover, ensuring ample space facilitates easy maneuverability for caretaking activities.

Individual Plant Breathing Room: Beyond rows, individual plants need their space. This space varies drastically from a compact lettuce to a sprawling tomato plant, necessitating differential spacing.

Recognizing Growth Patterns

Horizontal vs. Vertical Expansion: Some plants, like cucumbers, can spread outwards, consuming significant ground space. However, using trellises, they can be trained to grow vertically, thereby economizing on space.

Underground Considerations: Root crops may not always command horizontal space but can necessitate deeper soils to accommodate their downward growth.

The Strategy of Rotation and Succession

Crop Rotation Blueprint: Constantly planting the same crop can sap the soil of specific nutrients. Rotation ensures soil health, reduces pest infestations, and can even disrupt disease cycles.

Succession Planting: This is about timing. Once one crop is harvested, the same space can be immediately used for another crop, ensuring a continuous flow of produce.

DESIGNING AN EFFECTIVE AND EFFICIENT FARM LAYOUT

Classical Row Farming: While this might evoke images of expansive farms, even mini farms can benefit from this method, especially if there's a bit more room to play with. It's essential, though, to ensure that pathways between rows are sufficiently wide for easy access and any equipment use.

Square Foot Gardening: A more modern and space-efficient method, this divides the growing area into square-foot plots. Each section is dedicated to different crops based on their space requirements, leading to a neat, organized, and highly efficient setup.

Elevated Solutions – Raised Beds and Containers: Raised beds offer numerous advantages like enhanced drainage, demarcation, and the opportunity to use curated soil. On the other hand, containers offer portability and are ideal for spaces like balconies or terraces.

Embracing Verticality:

Vertical farming, a testament to human ingenuity, uses vertical space. Through trellises, stacked planters, or wall-mounted solutions, crops can be made to grow upwards, conserving ground space.

Synergistic Planting – Polyculture and Companions: Nature often works in tandem. Some plants, when grown together, can benefit each other, either by enhancing growth, deterring pests, or even improving flavor.

Sustainable Design with Permaculture: Inspired by natural ecosystems, permaculture integrates various layers of plants, from deep-rooted to tall aerial ones, ensuring optimal space usage and sustainability.

Factoring in Zoning and Microclimates: Every farm, no matter how small, will have pockets of microclimates. Recognizing these and zoning crops based on their needs and the care frequency they demand can further optimize the layout.

THE CYCLE OF OBSERVATION AND REFINEMENT

Continuous Supervision: Farms are dynamic. Observing how crops grow, noting if they are too cramped or too isolated, and adjusting in subsequent cycles is key.

Harvest as Feedback: Yields can offer insights. Are the crops thriving? Is the quality good? These observations can guide future layout decisions.

Vigilance Against Pests and Diseases: Layout can inadvertently impact pest prevalence or disease spread. Ensuring good airflow by avoiding overcrowding, for instance, can mitigate fungal infestations.

TECHNOLOGY AS AN ALLY IN LAYOUT PLANNING

Digital Farming Tools: Several apps and software can help simulate and design garden layouts, considering plant dimensions and growth propensities.

Eyes in the Sky – Drones: Drones provide a bird's eye view, which can be invaluable in spotting layout inefficiencies or issues that might not be apparent at ground level.

Sensing the Ground: Sensors can relay real-time data about soil moisture, helping make informed irrigation decisions based on the layout.

TAPPING INTO COLLECTIVE KNOWLEDGE

Local Farm Visits: Seeing is believing. Observing neighboring farms can offer insights, inspiration, and lessons.

Capacity Building through Training: Agricultural bodies often host training sessions, imparting knowledge tailored to regional specifics.

Digital Farmer Forums: Online platforms can be gold mines of shared experiences, innovative solutions, and community support.

In the mini farming every decision, every layout choice, every crop size consideration becomes a stitch that either strengthens or weakens the fabric. While the world of farming is ever-evolving, buoyed by new technologies and methodologies, the foundational tenets remain unchanged. Understanding the symbiotic relationship between the land and its crops, and then nurturing this relationship through thoughtful decisions, paves the way for a flourishing mini farm.

THE ESSENCE OF PROPORTION AND DIMENSION PLANNING

In the mini farming it's paramount to treat space as a premium asset. This requires a meticulous understanding of crop proportions and dimensions, ensuring that every square inch of your farm real estate is leveraged efficiently.

UNDERSTANDING CROP DIMENSIONS: BASICS TO BEGIN WITH

Every crop, from the tiniest herbs to the largest vegetables, has a unique spatial footprint. This footprint can be broken down into two primary components:

- **Above-ground dimensions:** This pertains to the space a plant will occupy horizontally (its spread) and vertically (its height).

- **Below-ground dimensions:** This refers to the depth and spread of roots.

When selecting crops for your mini farm, understanding and anticipating these dimensions ensures that plants have adequate space to thrive without inhibiting their neighbors.

DECODING ABOVE-GROUND DIMENSIONS

Leafy Vegetables: Crops like lettuce, spinach, and kale primarily have a horizontal spread. Typically, they require about 6-12 inches of space on all sides, depending on the variety.

Fruiting Vegetables: Tomatoes, peppers, and eggplants are examples of crops that grow taller. They require staking or caging to support their growth. Depending on the variety, tomatoes can spread 2-4 feet horizontally and grow up to 6 feet tall.

Vines and Climbers: Crops like beans, cucumbers, and peas can be trained to grow vertically on trellises, poles, or fences. While they might spread horizontally if left untrained, vertical training can economize space.

Grains: If you're considering grains like corn, they grow tall and need space both above and below ground. A corn plant might need a 12-inch spacing from its neighbors to flourish.

DECODING BELOW-GROUND DIMENSIONS

Shallow Rooted: Leafy vegetables, onions, and many herbs have shallow root systems, only requiring 6-12 inches of soil depth.

Medium Rooted: Crops like beans, cucumbers, and tomatoes need a bit more depth, usually 12-18 inches, to accommodate their root systems.

Deep Rooted: Root crops, such as carrots and potatoes, as well as some fruiting trees or shrubs, can require 24 inches or more soil depth.

EFFICIENTLY USING THE VERTICAL DIMENSION

Vertical farming isn't just for urban setups; it's a potent strategy for mini farms. Trellises, poles, and vertical planters can accommodate crops that have a natural tendency to climb or can be trained to do so.

Trellising Options: There are various designs available, from A-frame to single-pole structures. When designing, factor in the material's durability and the ease with which plants can latch onto them.

Height Management: While using vertical space is excellent, ensure you can access the crops, especially during harvesting. Tools like long-handled pruners might be required for very tall setups.

UNDERSTANDING THE INFLUENCE OF SPACING

Beyond individual crop dimensions, spacing plays a pivotal role in the health and productivity of your mini farm.

Row Spacing: This determines how rows of crops are aligned. Wider rows can facilitate movement and sometimes machinery. For densely planted crops, consider at least an 18-inch spacing between rows.

Plant Spacing: This is dictated by the individual plant's mature size. Overcrowding can stifle growth, reduce yield, and encourage pests or diseases.

Optimal Density: The aim is to achieve a canopy of leaves that can capture sunlight efficiently but still allow airflow to reduce fungal diseases.

PLANNING FOR CROP ROTATION

Crop rotation, even in a mini farm setup, offers myriad benefits, including improved soil health and reduced pest issues. When planning rotation:

Group Crops by Family: For instance, tomatoes, peppers, and eggplants are part of the nightshade family and have similar nutrient requirements and pest susceptibilities.

Sequential Planning: After a root vegetable, consider planting a leafy one. This not only diversifies the soil nutrient extraction but also mitigates pest carryover.

HARNESSING SUCCESSION PLANTING FOR CONTINUOUS YIELDS

Succession planting is the practice of planting new crops in spaces vacated by harvested ones. This ensures a continuous supply and optimal space usage.

Short Cycle Crops: Radishes, lettuces, and spinach have short growth cycles and can be successively planted several times within a season.

Staggered Planting: Instead of planting an entire bed of lettuce at once, stagger the planting over several weeks. This ensures not all plants mature at once, providing a prolonged harvest window.

IRRIGATION AND LAYOUT SYNERGY

Water is life, and its efficient distribution across your farm is crucial. When designing your mini farm:

Drip Irrigation: This system delivers water directly to the plant roots, conserving water and ensuring plants receive adequate moisture. The layout must accommodate the tubing and emitters.

Raised Beds and Drainage: If using raised beds, ensure the layout provides efficient drainage, especially during heavy rainfall.

INTERPLAY OF LIGHT AND LAYOUT

Sunlight is a crucial determinant in the growth of plants.

Track the Sun: Understand the sun's trajectory over your farm. This will help in placing taller crops in areas where they won't shade the shorter ones.

Manage Shade: Some crops benefit from partial shade, especially in hotter climates. Use taller plants or infrastructure like pergolas to create shade for these crops.

INTEGRATED PEST MANAGEMENT AND LAYOUT DESIGN

Natural Barriers: Plants like marigolds can deter certain pests. Interspersing such plants can create natural barriers against pest invasions.

Beneficial Insects: Plants like yarrow or fennel can attract beneficial insects that prey on pests. Factoring them into your layout can serve as a natural pest control strategy.

TECHNOLOGY AIDS IN LAYOUT DESIGN

While traditional wisdom is invaluable, modern tools can enhance precision in layout planning.

Digital Layout Tools: Software can simulate your farm space, allowing you to experiment with layouts before physically implementing them.

Soil Sensors: They can guide you on moisture levels, ensuring your layout provides adequate irrigation pathways for all crops.

LEVERAGING COMMUNITY WISDOM

Farm Tours: Regularly visiting other mini farms can offer fresh perspectives and insights on efficient layouts and crop dimensioning strategies.

Workshops and Training: Many agricultural bodies conduct workshops that can upskill you in the nuances of modern mini farming techniques.

In sum, designing a mini farm is both a science and an art. Every choice made, from crop selection to layout design, holds the potential to maximize yield, ensure crop health, and optimize resource usage. While this chapter provides foundational principles, continuous learning, observation, and adaptation will steer the farm towards unbridled success.

UNDERSTANDING THE FUNDAMENTALS OF CROP ROTATION

Crop rotation is the practice of growing different crops in succession on the same piece of land in sequential seasons. This age-old agricultural technique has several benefits: it prevents the buildup of pests that target specific crop families, reduces soil-borne diseases, and aids in maintaining soil structure and nutrient levels.

WHY CROP ROTATION MATTERS

Soil Fertility Management: Different crops extract and deposit varied nutrients in the soil. By rotating crops, farmers can naturally replenish nutrients that the preceding crop might have depleted.

Pest and Disease Control: Certain pests and diseases are crop-specific. Changing crops each season disrupts their lifecycle, reducing their populations without excessive use of chemical treatments.

Soil Erosion Prevention: Some crops, particularly those with robust root systems, can help prevent soil erosion. Rotating with such crops can ensure soil structure integrity.

Weed Management: Some crops can outcompete or suppress weed growth. Incorporating them in a rotation can naturally keep weeds at bay.

CATEGORIZING CROPS FOR EFFECTIVE ROTATION

Before delving into rotation strategies, it's essential to understand the various crop categories:

Legumes: These crops, including beans, peas, and lentils, have the unique ability to fix atmospheric nitrogen in the soil, benefiting subsequent crops.

Leafy Greens and Brassicas: Crops like lettuce, spinach, kale, broccoli, and cauliflower mainly extract nitrogen from the soil to support their lush growth.

Fruiting Vegetables: This group includes tomatoes, peppers, cucumbers, and squashes. They have substantial nutrient needs and can be more demanding on the soil.

Root Crops: Carrots, beets, turnips, and potatoes primarily draw nutrients from deeper soil layers.

BASIC CROP ROTATION FRAMEWORKS

A simple and effective approach to crop rotation is to utilize a 4-year rotation plan, aligned with the crop categories:

- ☐ **Year 1 - Legumes:** Starting with legumes ensures that the soil receives a good dose of nitrogen.

- ☐ **Year 2 - Leafy Greens and Brassicas:** These will benefit from the nitrogen boost provided by the legumes.

- ☐ **Year 3 - Fruiting Vegetables:** By now, the soil is primed with a mix of nutrients, meeting the demands of these crops.

- ☐ **Year 4 - Root Crops:** Diving deeper, these will use the lower nutrient profile remaining and prep the soil for the cycle to restart.

ADVANCED CROP ROTATION CONSIDERATIONS

Soil Health Indicators: Continually monitor soil health using tests that measure nutrient levels, pH, and microbial activity. These tests can guide tweaks in your rotation plan.

Pest and Disease Observations: Document any pest or disease outbreaks, including their severity and timing. This can provide insights into potential crop rotations that could mitigate future outbreaks.

Climatic Conditions: Weather patterns play a role in crop success. If a particular year is forecasted to have conditions unfavorable for a specific crop category, consider adjusting your rotation.

INTERPLANTING AND RELAY PLANTING IN ROTATION

Interplanting: This involves growing two or more crops together in close proximity. While not pure rotation, it operates on similar principles. For instance, planting beans (a legume) with corn (a grass) can provide mutual benefits. The beans fix nitrogen, aiding the corn, while the corn stalks offer the beans natural trellises.

Relay Planting: This is the process of planting a new crop before the existing one is harvested. For instance, planting lettuce in between young tomato plants. By the time the tomatoes need more space, the lettuce is harvested.

COVER CROPS AND GREEN MANURES IN ROTATION

Cover Crops: These are typically fast-growing crops that cover bare soil between rotations. They protect against erosion, suppress weeds, and can improve soil structure. Examples include clover, buckwheat, and ryegrass.

Green Manures: Often used interchangeably with cover crops, green manures are plants grown specifically to be incorporated back into the soil. Their decomposition adds organic matter and nutrients to the soil.

MANAGING PERSISTENT PESTS AND DISEASES

Even with impeccable rotation, some pests and diseases can persist. In such scenarios:

Extended Rotation: If a particular pest targets potatoes, for example, consider growing potatoes less frequently than the standard rotation.

Biofumigation: Some crops release compounds that suppress pests and diseases. Incorporating mustard or certain brassicas can reduce nematode populations in the soil.

Natural Predators: Encourage the presence of beneficial insects and animals. Ladybugs, lacewings, and birds can keep pest populations in check.

CROP ROTATION AND SOIL TILLAGE

The way soil is tilled or managed can influence the success of crop rotation.

No-Till Farming: This approach leaves the soil undisturbed, preserving its structure. It works well with crop rotation by allowing the natural decomposition of plant residues, further enriching the soil.

Reduced Tillage: Instead of extensive plowing, this method lightly turns the soil. It can help incorporate the residues of leguminous crops, expediting the nitrogen-fixation process.

INCORPORATING PERENNIALS IN ROTATION

While crop rotation primarily focuses on annuals, perennials can play a part.

Perennial Legumes: Crops like alfalfa or clover can be grown for multiple years. They continuously fix nitrogen and can serve as an anchor in your rotation cycle.

Orchards and Agroforestry: If part of your mini farm includes fruit trees or woody shrubs, understand their influence on soil nutrients. The fallen leaves or pruned branches can contribute organic matter.

TOOLS AND TECHNOLOGY IN CROP ROTATION

Crop Rotation Software: Numerous digital platforms can assist in planning rotations, considering factors like soil health, climate forecasts, and historical pest data.

Drones and Sensors: A bird's-eye view from drones can offer insights into crop health, signaling potential soil nutrient imbalances. Soil sensors can provide real-time data on moisture and nutrient levels.

LEARNING FROM TRADITION, ADAPTING TO MODERN CHALLENGES

Historical Practices: Many traditional farming communities have practiced crop rotation for centuries. Their empirical knowledge can offer invaluable insights.

Modern Research: Stay abreast of the latest research. Agricultural institutions continually study crop rotation, and their findings can.

CHAPTER 3

SUSTAINABLE AGRICULTURAL TECHNIQUES

THE CORE COMPONENTS OF SOIL

Soil, often termed as the Earth's living skin, is more than just dirt under our feet. It's a complex mixture that sustains life. A thorough understanding of its components aids in sustainable farming.

Mineral Particles: These constitute the sand, silt, and clay in the soil, forming its texture. Their relative proportions define the soil type, which in turn affects water retention and aeration.

Organic Matter: This encompasses decomposed plants, animals, and microorganisms. Organic matter enriches the soil with essential nutrients and enhances its structure.

Water: Soil water, containing dissolved minerals and nutrients, is crucial for plant uptake. Its quantity varies with soil type, organic content, and climatic conditions.

Air: The spaces between soil particles contain air, which provides oxygen to plant roots and soil organisms.

Living Organisms: From bacteria, fungi, and protozoa to worms, insects, and plant roots, a myriad of life forms call soil their home. They play critical roles in nutrient cycling and soil structure.

SOIL PH AND ITS IMPLICATIONS

Soil pH measures the acidity or alkalinity of the soil. It affects nutrient availability, microbial activity, and overall soil health.

Understanding the Scale: The pH scale ranges from 0 to 14. A pH of 7 is neutral, values below 7 indicate acidity, and those above 7 denote alkalinity.

Influence on Nutrient Availability: Some nutrients are more available in acidic conditions, while others thrive in alkaline settings. Extreme pH levels can limit nutrient uptake by plants.

Modifying Soil pH: If the soil pH isn't optimal for the crops being cultivated, it can be adjusted. Lime or wood ash can raise pH (reduce acidity), while sulfur or certain organic mulches can lower pH (increase acidity).

ORGANIC MATTER: THE HEARTBEAT OF SOIL

Benefits of Organic Matter: It enhances soil structure, improves water retention, boosts nutrient content, and promotes microbial life.

Sources: Compost, manure, leaf mold, and green manures are valuable sources. Regularly incorporating these can steadily increase the soil's organic content.

Decomposition: As organic matter breaks down, it releases nutrients in plant-accessible forms. This natural nutrient cycling reduces the need for synthetic fertilizers.

SOIL EROSION: CAUSES AND MITIGATION

Understanding Erosion: It's the removal of the topsoil layer due to wind, water, or human activity. This layer is rich in organic matter and vital for crop growth.

Preventive Techniques:

☐ **Cover Cropping:** Fast-growing crops, sown during off-seasons, protect the soil surface.

☐ **Contour Plowing:** Tilling along the natural contours of the land reduces soil displacement.

☐ **Agroforestry:** Introducing trees and shrubs can act as windbreaks and anchor the soil with their roots.

THE ROLE OF MICROBES IN SOIL HEALTH

Symbiotic Relationships: Many plants form symbiotic relationships with fungi (mycorrhizae) and bacteria. Legumes, for instance, house nitrogen-fixing bacteria in their root nodules.

Decomposers: Microbes break down organic matter, facilitating nutrient cycling.

Disease Suppression: Beneficial microbes can suppress or outcompete pathogenic organisms, acting as a natural defense.

SOIL COMPACTION: RECOGNIZING AND ADDRESSING

Causes: Heavy machinery, overgrazing, or frequent tilling can lead to compaction. This results in reduced air spaces, limiting root growth and microbial activity.

MITIGATION STRATEGIES:

Deep Rooted Crops: Plants like daikon radish can naturally break up compacted layers.

Reduced or No-Till Farming: Limiting soil disturbance can prevent compaction.

THE IMPORTANCE OF SOIL TESTING

Parameters Tested: Nutrient levels, pH, organic matter content, and certain contaminants are commonly assessed.

Frequency: While annual testing is beneficial, at a minimum, tests should be done every 3-4 years or when noticeable plant health issues arise.

Interpreting Results: Soil tests often provide recommendations for amendments. It's crucial to interpret these with sustainable practices in mind, prioritizing organic and natural inputs.

NATURAL SOIL AMENDMENTS FOR NUTRIENT MANAGEMENT

Compost: Rich in a variety of nutrients and improves soil structure.

Worm Castings: These are the excreta of earthworms, packed with nutrients in a readily available form for plants.

Bone Meal and Blood Meal: Organic sources of phosphorus and nitrogen, respectively.

Seaweed and Kelp: Provide a range of micronutrients and growth-promoting substances.

WATER MANAGEMENT IN SOIL

Mulching: Applying organic material like straw or leaves on the soil surface conserves moisture, suppresses weeds, and adds organic matter as it decomposes.

Drip Irrigation: Delivers water directly to plant roots, reducing evaporation losses and preventing surface runoff.

REGENERATIVE AGRICULTURE AND SOIL HEALTH

Regenerative agriculture emphasizes practices that restore and enhance soil health.

Cover Cropping and Green Manures: Beyond preventing erosion, they add organic matter and assist in nutrient cycling.

Crop Rotation and Polyculture: These enhance soil health by preventing nutrient depletion and breaking pest and disease cycles.

Agroecology: This holistic approach considers the farm as an ecosystem. It prioritizes biodiversity, both above and below ground, recognizing its role in resilience and productivity.

THE FUTURE: SOIL MICROBIOME RESEARCH

Recent years have witnessed an increased focus on understanding the soil microbiome—the vast community of microbes in the soil.

Soil DNA Sequencing: By analyzing soil DNA, researchers can identify the microbial species present and their functions.

Applications: Insights from such research can guide practices to foster beneficial microbes, offering solutions to agricultural challenges.

TOOLS AND TECHNOLOGY IN SOIL MANAGEMENT

Soil Moisture Sensors: These provide real-time data on soil water content, assisting in precise irrigation.

Remote Sensing and Drones: They can detect variations in soil health across a farm, highlighting areas needing attention.

Digital Platforms: Numerous software solutions aid in soil data analysis, helping farmers make informed decisions.

MAINTAINING SOIL HEALTH IN URBAN AND PERI-URBAN AGRICULTURE

Urban settings pose unique challenges and opportunities for soil management.

Raised Beds and Containers: These can bypass contaminated or poor-quality urban soils. Fill them with a balanced mix of compost, loam, and other components.

Vermiculture: In space-constrained settings, worm composting can efficiently process organic waste, producing rich worm castings for soil enrichment.

In the realm of sustainable agriculture, understanding and maintaining soil health is paramount. The practices outlined above, rooted in both traditional wisdom and modern research, offer a roadmap to ensure that the soil continues to sustain life for generations to come.

UNDERSTANDING THE TENETS OF ORGANIC FARMING

Organic farming isn't simply a set of techniques; it embodies a philosophy that seeks harmony between man, earth, and the myriad organisms that share our environment.

Avoidance of Synthetic Inputs: Organic farming strictly limits the use of synthetic fertilizers, pesticides, herbicides, and genetically modified organisms (GMOs). Instead, it focuses on natural inputs and methods.

Emphasis on Soil Health: Central to organic farming is the belief in "feeding the soil, not the plant." Organic practices, like composting, cover cropping, and green manures, enhance soil fertility and structure.

Biological Pest and Disease Management: Instead of synthetic pesticides, organic farming relies on biological controls like beneficial insects, birds, and companion planting to manage pests and diseases.

Crop Diversity: Organic farms often grow a variety of crops, embracing crop rotation and polyculture. This not only boosts soil health but also reduces pest and disease pressures.

Animal and Plant Integration: Livestock, when managed well, play a role in organic systems by providing manure, controlling pests, and improving soil structure.

FUNDAMENTAL PRINCIPLES OF PERMACULTURE

Permaculture is a design science that seeks to mimic nature's patterns and relationships to create sustainable and regenerative agricultural systems.

Observe and Interact: Before acting, one must observe. This involves understanding the land, its patterns, and the inherent relationships between its elements.

Catch and Store Energy: This principle is about harnessing nature's bounty. From rainwater harvesting systems to planting deciduous trees for summer shade, it's about optimizing the natural energy and resources available.

Obtain a Yield: Ensure that your systems produce results. While long-term sustainability is a goal, short-term outputs are essential for immediate sustenance and motivation.

Apply Self-Regulation and Accept Feedback: Nature thrives on feedback loops. Similarly, constantly monitor your systems, learn from successes and failures, and adjust accordingly.

Use and Value Renewable Resources: From solar energy to wind power, sustainable systems prioritize renewable over finite resources.

Produce No Waste: In nature, waste from one organism becomes food for another. Aim to mimic this cyclical pattern by reusing, recycling, and integrating system outputs.

Design from Patterns to Details: Look at nature's patterns, like the branching of trees or the flow of water, and replicate them in your designs. Only then should you focus on specific system details.

Integrate Rather Than Segregate: In nature, cooperative relationships often dominate. Design systems where elements support and enhance each other, rather than existing in isolation.

Use Small and Slow Solutions: Bigger isn't always better. Small systems are often easier to manage and more resilient to failures.

Use and Value Diversity: Just as monocultures are vulnerable in nature, they are in designed systems too. Diversity brings strength, resilience, and increased yields.

Use Edges and Value the Marginal: The interface between different systems or habitats often houses unique species and interactions. Embrace these "edge" areas and the opportunities they offer.

Creatively Use and Respond to Change: Change is inevitable. Instead of resisting it, understand it, predict it, and turn it to your advantage.

ORGANIC FARMING TECHNIQUES AND PRACTICES

Cover Cropping: These are non-commercial crops grown to suppress weeds, manage soil erosion, help build and improve soil fertility, and control pests and diseases.

Natural Pest Control: This involves techniques such as introducing predatory insects, creating habitats for natural predators, and interplanting to confuse pests.

Composting: This is the process of converting organic waste into rich, fertile humus for enriching the soil.

Agroforestry: Combining trees, shrubs, and crops in a system can provide diverse yields, stabilize the soil, and support a diverse ecosystem.

PERMACULTURE DESIGN TECHNIQUES

Zoning: This means positioning elements based on the frequency of human use and plant or animal needs. For instance, frequently harvested vegetables might be closer (Zone 1) to the home, while a wilder woodland may be farther away (Zone 5).

Layering: Mimicking Forest layers, from canopy trees to ground-cover plants, can maximize yield in a given space.

Guilds: These are groupings of plants, animals, and insects that work together, supporting each other's health and productivity.

Swales: Contour-based ditches that capture rainwater runoff, allowing it to infiltrate and hydrate the landscape.

Keyhole Gardens: An efficient, energy-saving garden design that minimizes walking space and maximizes planting area.

THE ROLE OF ANIMALS IN ORGANIC AND PERMACULTURE SYSTEMS

Chickens: Beyond providing eggs and meat, they can be instrumental in pest control, composting, and even tilling.

Cows and Goats: Their manure is a rich fertilizer, and they can be part of managed grazing systems that mimic natural herbivore movements, rejuvenating pastures and sequestering carbon.

Bees: Crucial for pollination, they also provide honey, wax, and other valuable products.

Ducks: Excellent for pest control, especially slugs, they also provide eggs and meat.

ORGANIC CERTIFICATION: THE HOW AND WHY

Standards and Regulations: Each country has its standards for organic production, often overseen by government agencies or recognized certifying bodies.

The Certification Process: Typically involves an initial assessment, regular inspections, and adherence to organic standards.

Market Benefits: Organic certification can provide market access, premium prices, and consumer trust.

THE INTERSECTION OF ORGANIC AND PERMACULTURE

While organic farming often focuses on the "no" (no chemicals, no GMOs), permaculture is more about the "how." It's about designing systems. They both aim for sustainability, but permaculture takes a broader view, considering not just agricultural production, but also energy, shelter, and other human needs within its design scope. Integrating both can offer a comprehensive approach to truly sustainable farming.

CHALLENGES AND REWARDS

Every farming system has its challenges. Organic farmers might grapple with pest outbreaks, while permaculturists may need to adjust designs that don't initially work. However, the rewards, from healthier soils and ecosystems to more resilient food systems and communities, make the journey worthwhile.

CONTINUED EDUCATION AND COMMUNITY ENGAGEMENT

Workshops: Regularly attending workshops can keep you updated with the latest organic and permaculture techniques.

Farm Tours: Visiting other farms can offer fresh perspectives and insights.

Networking: Engaging with a community of like-minded individuals can provide support, advice, and camaraderie.

Organic farming and permaculture aren't mere techniques; they're holistic approaches to agriculture that emphasize sustainability, resilience, and harmony with nature. By understanding their principles and practices, modern farmers can chart a path that not only ensures productivity but also safeguards the environment and community well-being.

THE IMPERATIVE OF WATER CONSERVATION IN MODERN AGRICULTURE

Water is the lifeblood of agriculture. With the increasing frequency of droughts, erratic rainfall, and depleting groundwater levels, conserving water in farming isn't just an environmental concern—it's an economic and societal necessity. Modern farmers must embrace a holistic approach to water management that ensures crop productivity while minimizing wastage and ensuring long-term sustainability.

UNDERSTANDING WATER USE IN AGRICULTURE

Transpiration: The process by which water is taken up by plant roots, moves through plants, and evaporates into the atmosphere from plant leaves.

Evaporation: The transformation of water from liquid to gas, often from soil surfaces and water bodies.

Infiltration: The process of water soaking into the soil.

Runoff: Excess water that flows over the ground surface when the soil is saturated.

EFFICIENT IRRIGATION TECHNIQUES

Drip Irrigation: Delivers water directly to the root zone of plants, minimizing evaporation losses. It's especially suitable for high-value crops and water-scarce areas.

Soaker Hoses: These porous hoses deliver water to the soil's surface, reducing evaporation while ensuring even watering.

Sprinkler Irrigation: Suitable for large areas, modern sprinklers are designed to mimic natural rainfall and can be adjusted to control the rate, amount, and area of coverage.

Subsurface Irrigation: A system where water is delivered below the soil surface, directly to the root zone, minimizing surface evaporation.

Rainwater Harvesting: Collecting and storing rainwater in tanks or ponds for future use. With proper filtration, it can be an excellent source for irrigation.

MULCHING AND SOIL CONSERVATION

Benefits of Mulching: Mulching conserves moisture, reduces evaporation, suppresses weeds, and improves soil health.

Types of Mulch:

- **Organic Mulch:** Includes straw, leaves, wood chips, and compost. It decomposes over time, enriching the soil.

- **Inorganic Mulch:** Includes plastic films or landscape fabric. Especially effective for weed suppression and moisture retention.

Cover Crops: Plants grown to cover and protect the soil. They improve soil structure, enhance infiltration, reduce evaporation, and minimize runoff.

MANAGING SOIL TO ENHANCE WATER RETENTION

Organic Matter: Adding compost, manure, or green manure increases the soil's water-holding capacity.

Soil Structure: Well-aggregated soil promotes infiltration and reduces surface runoff. Regular organic inputs and reduced tillage can promote a good structure.

Soil Depth: Deeper soils can store more water. Practices like deep ripping can be used to break hardpans and enhance root depth.

NATURAL LANDSCAPING AND DRY FARMING

Native Plants: These are adapted to local conditions and often require less water than introduced species.

Dry Farming: Relies on the moisture stored in the soil from the rainy season to grow crops during drier months. It emphasizes deep rooting and soil preparation.

MONITORING AND MANAGING WATER USE

Soil Moisture Sensors: These devices can provide real-time data on soil moisture levels, helping farmers irrigate more efficiently.

Weather Predictions: Modern forecasting can help farmers anticipate rainfall and adjust irrigation accordingly.

Water Meters: Useful in monitoring water usage, helping in waste reduction.

WATER-SAVING PRACTICES AROUND THE FARM

Regular Maintenance: Periodically check and repair the irrigation system to prevent leaks and wastage.

Optimal Watering Times: Watering during cooler parts of the day (early morning or late evening) can reduce evaporation losses.

Conservation Tillage: Techniques like no-till or reduced till can improve soil structure, enhancing its water retention capabilities.

Managing Farm Ponds: Ensure they are shaded or covered to minimize evaporation. Using them as reservoirs for rainwater or runoff can be beneficial.

AQUAPONICS AND HYDROPONICS: A WATER-EFFICIENT FUTURE

Aquaponics: A system combining aquaculture (raising fish) and hydroponics (soilless plant culture). The fish waste provides nutrients for the plants, while plants help filter and purify the water.

Hydroponics: Growing plants in nutrient-rich water solutions. It can save up to 90% of the water used in traditional farming.

LEGISLATION AND WATER RIGHTS

Water Allocation: Many regions have laws governing water use for agriculture, ensuring equitable distribution and conservation.

Incentives for Conservation: Some governments provide subsidies or incentives for adopting water-saving technologies or practices.

ENGAGING WITH THE COMMUNITY

Knowledge Sharing: Farmers can benefit from sharing experiences and techniques related to water conservation.

Collective Action: Communities can come together to build shared infrastructure like check dams, ponds, or rainwater harvesting systems.

GLOBAL PERSPECTIVE ON WATER CONSERVATION

Virtual Water Trade: It's the amount of water embedded in the production of goods and services. Recognizing this can help in making sustainable trade decisions.

Global Initiatives: International bodies, NGOs, and governments are working collaboratively to address the global water crisis in agriculture.

Water conservation in agriculture is a multifaceted challenge requiring a blend of traditional wisdom, innovative techniques, and community engagement. As stewards of the land, modern farmers have a pivotal role in shaping sustainable water management practices, ensuring not just the prosperity of their farms, but the health and vitality of entire ecosystems.

THE SCIENCE OF ORGANIC MATTER DECOMPOSITION

When we speak of compost, we talk about a complex process powered by millions of microorganisms that facilitate the breakdown of organic matter. The science of composting is not just decay; it's a harmonious dance between organic materials and the organisms breaking them down.

DECOMPOSITION DYNAMICS UNVEILED

Bacteria's Role: They're the primary decomposers, with different strains thriving at varying temperature ranges. From psychrophilic bacteria in colder temperatures to thermophilic strains in hotter conditions, they sequentially play a role in breaking down complex organic molecules.

Contribution of Fungi: Fungi, including molds and yeast, tackle the more challenging components, including those with high cellulose and lignin content, giving a thorough decomposition of tougher materials.

Actinomycetes – The Bridge: Often mistaken for fungi due to their filamentous structure, they break down some of the more stubborn materials left behind by bacteria and fungi, playing a bridge role in the composting ecology.

A DEEP DIVE INTO AEROBIC AND ANAEROBIC COMPOSTING

While both are natural processes, the choice between aerobic and anaerobic composting will determine the speed, quality, and characteristics of the end product.

Aerobic Composting: Relying on oxygen, this process encourages microorganisms that require air. It's generally faster and produces minimal odor when correctly managed. An added advantage is the heat generated, which can kill weed seeds and pathogens.

Anaerobic Composting: This method doesn't require turning, making it less labor-intensive. However, it's slower and can produce a distinct odor due to the different set of microorganisms at work.

TEMPERATURE: THE SILENT REGULATOR

Temperature doesn't just indicate the progress of composting; it also controls it. The various phases marked by different temperature ranges determine which microorganisms dominate and the kind of breakdown happening within.

Mesophilic Range: Here, general organic matter decomposition occurs, setting the stage for the thermophilic phase.

Thermophilic Range: This is where the magic happens. High temperatures ensure the destruction of pathogens and weed seeds, making the compost safer and more beneficial.

Cooling Phase: It's essential to let the compost cool and mature. This phase ensures the stability of the compost, making it ready for use without the risk of harming plants.

DESIGNING THE IDEAL COMPOST PILE: COMPONENTS MATTER

Each element in a compost pile has a purpose. It's not just about dumping organic waste; it's about creating the right environment for effective decomposition.

Carbon and Nitrogen – The Balancing Act: Too much carbon makes a slow-decomposing pile, while excessive nitrogen can produce ammonia gas. Striking a balance is crucial. A ratio of 25-30:1 (C:N) has been found optimal for microbial activity.

The Moisture Paradigm: While moisture is vital, too much can drown the microbes, and too little can halt the process. Achieving a moisture level akin to a wrung-out sponge ensures microbial activities aren't hindered.

Particle Size and Its Importance: The size of the materials in the pile influences decomposition speed. Smaller particles offer more surface area for microbes to work on. However, incorporating larger chunks can ensure adequate aeration throughout the pile.

METHODS AND SYSTEMS: TAILORING COMPOSTING TO NEEDS

Every farm, garden, or community has unique needs, and the composting system should cater to those.

Windrow vs. Static Pile: While windrows are optimal for large-scale composting, static piles can handle vast volumes with the right aeration system.

Bins and In-vessel Systems: For controlled environments or small-scale composting, bins and in-vessel systems can offer an efficient decomposition process with minimal space requirements.

The Magic of Vermicomposting: The humble earthworm, especially red wigglers, can transform organic waste into vermicast, a nutrient powerhouse. Vermicomposting isn't just about decomposition; it's about enhancing the end product's quality.

CHOOSING THE RIGHT MATERIALS: NOT ALL WASTE IS EQUAL

Different organic wastes bring different characteristics to the compost pile.

Green vs. Brown Materials: While green materials introduce nitrogen, brown materials are carbon sources. Balancing them is the key to an efficient compost pile.

Red Flags in Composting: Some materials might seem organic but can be detrimental. Diseased plants can introduce pathogens, and meat scraps can attract pests. Being selective ensures a healthy composting process.

ADVANCED TECHNIQUES FOR THE MODERN FARMER

While traditional composting has its merits, newer methods offer more control and efficiency.

Bokashi Composting: Fermentation at its best, this method relies on specific microorganisms to ferment organic waste, producing a unique compost variant.

Aerated Systems: Leveraging technology, aerated systems speed up composting by ensuring every part of the pile gets the required air, avoiding the labor-intensive turning process.

COMPOSTING: A PILLAR OF SUSTAINABLE AGRICULTURE

For the modern farmer, composting is not just a method—it's a philosophy. It aligns with the principles of sustainability, recycling, and holistic farming. By transforming waste into a resource, reducing dependency on synthetic inputs, and rejuvenating the soil, composting stands as a testament to nature's ability to heal and nourish.

The modern agricultural landscape is evolving, with an increasing emphasis on practices that support long-term sustainability. Composting, with its myriad benefits, plays a pivotal role in shaping this future, turning challenges into opportunities and waste into wealth.

PEST AND DISEASE CONTROL AND PREVENTION

DIVING DEEPER INTO INTEGRATED PEST MANAGEMENT (IPM)

Integrated Pest Management (IPM) is not merely a methodology but a comprehensive approach that encompasses a spectrum of strategies and techniques. At the core of IPM is the philosophy of reducing reliance on chemical interventions and leveraging an array of sustainable methods for holistic management.

Elements of IPM:

- **Threshold Levels:** It's essential to determine the levels at which pests become economically harmful. Not every pest presence warrants intervention. The decision to manage pests should ideally be based on their numbers exceeding an established threshold.

- **Regular Monitoring:** Systematic and consistent observation of crops ensures early detection, which is pivotal for timely and effective interventions. Monitoring tools can range from simple visual inspections to sophisticated devices like pheromone traps.

- **Strategic Interventions:** The heart of IPM is the integration of multiple strategies— biological, cultural, mechanical, and, if indispensable, chemical. The synergy between these methods can drastically diminish pest populations.

ADVANCING CULTURAL CONTROL TECHNIQUES

Beyond merely altering the environment, cultural controls delve into the roots of sustainable farming, emphasizing practices that inherently reduce the risk of pests and diseases.

Intercropping: Growing two or more crops simultaneously in proximity can deter pests. The presence of multiple crops can disrupt the host-finding ability of pests. Moreover, some crops can act as trap crops, luring pests away from the main crop.

Timing of Planting: Adjusting sowing dates can help evade peak pest periods. By understanding the life cycle of a pest, farmers can strategically time their planting to minimize exposure to pest attacks.

Soil Health: Soil isn't just a medium for growing crops; it's a living ecosystem. Maintaining its health by adding organic matter and ensuring good drainage can bolster plants' resistance to pests and diseases.

UNVEILING THE POWER OF BIOLOGICAL CONTROL

Biological control, in essence, is nature's way of keeping pests in check. By harnessing nature's predators, parasites, and pathogens, farmers can achieve substantial pest control.

Predators: These are organisms that prey on pests. For instance, spiders, ladybugs, and lacewings actively consume aphids, thereby reducing their populations.

Parasitoids: These organisms lay their eggs in or on pests. When the eggs hatch, the emerging larvae feed on the pest, eventually killing it. Examples include certain wasps that parasitize caterpillars.

Pathogens: Bacteria, fungi, and viruses can cause diseases in pests, leading to their decline. A classic example is the bacterium *Bacillus thuringiensis*, which is lethal to several insect pests.

THE MECHANICS OF MECHANICAL AND PHYSICAL CONTROLS

These controls are direct interventions that either remove pests from the environment or create barriers to protect plants.

Insect Netting: Fine mesh nets can prevent pests like the cabbage moth from accessing crops, thus averting potential damage.

Soil Solarization: This technique involves covering moist soil with clear plastic during the hottest part of the year. The resultant heat can kill soil-borne pathogens and pests.

Sticky Traps: These traps, often colored yellow or blue, attract and capture flying pests like whiteflies and fungus gnats.

CHEMICAL CONTROLS: TREADING CAREFULLY

While sustainable agriculture strives to minimize chemical use, there are situations where they become essential. The emphasis, however, is on precision, selectivity, and safety.

Botanicals: These plant-derived chemicals, like neem and pyrethrum, are biodegradable and generally less harmful to non-target organisms.

Microbial Pesticides: These are microorganisms that target specific pests without harming beneficial insects. Spinosad, derived from a naturally occurring bacterium, is effective against caterpillars, thrips, and many other pests.

Insect Growth Regulators (IGRs): IGRs disrupt the growth and development of pests, ensuring they don't mature to reproductive stages. Being specific to certain pests, they generally have minimal impact on beneficial insects.

A DEEP DIVE INTO DISEASE RESISTANCE AND BIOLOGICAL CONTROLS

Nature has equipped plants with mechanisms to fend off diseases. By understanding and capitalizing on these natural defenses, farmers can significantly reduce disease incidence.

Induced Resistance: Certain beneficial soil microorganisms, when in association with plant roots, can trigger the plant's defense mechanisms, making it less susceptible to diseases.

Antagonistic Organisms: Some microbes actively inhibit or kill pathogens. Trichoderma fungi, for instance, can colonize plant roots and protect them from soil-borne pathogens.

Resistant Cultivars: Breeding plants for disease resistance is a long-term and effective strategy. These cultivars possess genetic traits that either repel pathogens or reduce the impact of the disease.

WATER MANAGEMENT IN DISEASE CONTROL

Water, while essential for crops, can also be a conduit for disease spread. Proper water management, therefore, is integral for disease prevention.

Drip Irrigation: Delivering water directly to plant roots not only conserves water but also reduces foliage wetness, a condition favorable for many fungal diseases.

Mulching: Mulches, especially organic ones, prevent soil splash, which can transfer soil-borne pathogens to plant leaves.

Proper Spacing: Ensuring adequate spacing between plants improves air circulation, hastening leaf drying and reducing the chances of fungal and bacterial diseases.

LEVERAGING MODERN TECHNOLOGY

Embracing technology can enhance the efficiency and effectiveness of pest and disease control measures.

Remote Sensing: Satellites and drones equipped with sensors can detect pest or disease outbreaks even before they become visually apparent, allowing for early interventions.

Artificial Intelligence (AI): AI-driven tools can analyze data from various sources, like weather stations and remote sensing devices, to predict potential pest and disease outbreaks.

Digital Record Keeping: Using software tools, farmers can maintain detailed records of pest and disease incidences, interventions employed, and their outcomes. Such records are invaluable for refining strategies and ensuring continuous improvement.

EMPOWERING THROUGH TRAINING AND CAPACITY BUILDING

For sustainable techniques to be successfully implemented, farmers need to be well-informed and equipped with the requisite skills.

Digital Platforms: Webinars, online courses, and mobile applications can provide farmers with the latest insights and techniques in pest and disease control.

Demonstration Farms: These are farms where various sustainable techniques are actively practiced. They offer tangible evidence of the efficacy of these methods and serve as training hubs.

Farmer Field Schools: Here, farmers learn through doing. They experiment with different techniques, observe the outcomes, and make informed decisions based on their observations.

THE LARGER PICTURE: BIODIVERSITY AND ETHICAL CONSIDERATIONS

Sustainable pest and disease control is more than just about protecting crops; it's about preserving the intricate web of life.

Pollinators: Many of the practices that protect crops from pests also benefit pollinators. Avoiding broad-spectrum pesticides, for instance, ensures the survival of bees, which are pivotal for crop pollination.

Soil Life: Healthy soil teems with life—from bacteria and fungi to earthworms and beetles. Sustainable practices nurture this underground biodiversity, leading to robust crop growth.

Natural Predators: By minimizing chemical interventions, farmers ensure the survival of natural predators like spiders and beetles, which play a pivotal role in keeping pest populations in check.

In the evolving landscape of agriculture, where challenges are multifaceted, the approach to pest and disease control needs to be comprehensive, integrated, and rooted in sustainability. The confluence of traditional wisdom, modern science, and technological advancements offers promising pathways to protect crops, preserve the environment, and produce food that's safe and wholesome. The future of agriculture is undeniably sustainable, and every stakeholder, from the farmer to the consumer, has a role to play in this transformative journey.

BOOK 2

CHAPTER 4

GROWING IN LIMITED SPACES

VERTICAL GARDENS AND CONTAINER GARDENING TECHNIQUES

VERTICAL GARDENS: MAXIMIZING VERTICAL REAL ESTATE

The Concept of Vertical Gardening

Vertical gardening is a progressive approach to urban agriculture and landscape design, utilizing vertical spaces to cultivate plants. By growing plants upwards, on structures or specialized gardening systems, vertical gardens can transform underutilized spaces into verdant, productive, and aesthetic features.

Benefits of Vertical Gardening

Efficient Use of Space: Especially in urban settings with limited ground space, vertical gardens optimize the utilization of available area.

Enhanced Aesthetic Appeal: Vertical gardens, often termed as 'living walls,' can beautify structures, masking plain walls with vibrant plant life.

Improved Air Quality: Plants in vertical gardens can absorb pollutants, act as a biofilter, and release fresh oxygen.

Reduced Urban Heat Island Effect: Green walls can help in lowering ambient temperatures, providing a cooling effect in urbanized areas.

Potential for Increased Crop Yield: In agricultural contexts, growing crops vertically can, in some cases, lead to higher yields per square foot.

Types of Vertical Gardens

Trellis Systems: Simple and effective, these involve a latticed framework where plants, especially climbers, are trained to grow vertically.

Wall Planters: These are containers affixed to walls. They can be modular systems where individual plant containers hook together, creating a larger vertical display.

Green Walls: Sophisticated systems that integrate a growth medium directly onto the wall. These can be hydroponic, where plants receive nutrients from water, or they might incorporate soil or alternative mediums.

Tiered Planters: Stacked pots or containers, each holding different plants, maximizing the vertical space they occupy.

Vertical Pockets: Made from felt or similar materials, these pockets are mounted on walls and filled with soil, offering space for plants to grow.

Choice of Plants for Vertical Gardens

Climbing Plants: These naturally grow vertically, making them suitable for trellises and similar supports. Examples include ivy, jasmine, and passionfruit.

Epiphytes: Plants like certain ferns and orchids, which in nature often grow on other plants or trees, can be ideal for certain vertical systems.

Succulents: With their minimal water needs, succulents can thrive in vertical pocket systems.

Edible Plants: Many herbs, strawberries, and even certain vegetables like lettuce can adapt well to vertical gardening techniques.

Maintaining Soil and Nutrient Levels

Soil Volume: Ensure that the chosen system provides enough soil volume for plant roots to grow and spread.

Water Retention vs. Drainage: While the soil should retain enough moisture, avoid water stagnation, which can harm roots.

Nutrient Management: Vertical gardens, especially those with limited soil volume, might require regular feeding. Liquid fertilizers or slow-release granules can be effective.

Watering Vertical Gardens

Drip Irrigation: This efficient system delivers water directly to plant roots, minimizing wastage.

Automated Systems: For larger green walls, consider automated watering systems that are time or moisture-controlled.

Manual Watering: Smaller vertical setups might be watered manually using a watering can with a long spout for precision.

Pest and Disease Management

Regular Monitoring: Regularly inspect plants for signs of pests or diseases. Due to proximity, issues might spread faster in vertical gardens.

Natural Predators: Encourage beneficial insects like ladybugs or praying mantises which naturally control pest populations.

Pruning: Regularly prune dead or diseased plant parts to maintain the health of the vertical garden.

Structural and Weight Considerations

Weight Load: The combined weight of plants, soil, water, and the system itself can be substantial. Ensure the wall or structure can bear this load.

Anchoring Systems: Use robust anchoring systems, brackets, or frames to secure vertical gardens, especially in windy conditions.

Maintenance Access: Design the garden such that all plants are easily accessible for care and maintenance.

Optimizing Plant Growth

Sunlight Distribution: Ensure all plants receive adequate sunlight, considering the garden's orientation. In cases of insufficient light, consider using grow lights.

Pruning for Shape: Regularly prune plants to maintain the desired shape and density of the vertical garden.

Rotation Strategy: If certain plants aren't thriving in their position, consider rotating them with others to ensure uniform growth.

Sustainability in Vertical Gardens

Rainwater Harvesting: Integrate rainwater collection systems to provide a sustainable water source for the garden.

Recycled Materials: Consider using recycled or upcycled materials for planters, frames, or other components.

Native Plant Selection: Using native plants can enhance the garden's resilience, reduce water needs, and support local wildlife.

Vertical gardens offer a fusion of form and function. They merge aesthetics with productivity, making them a valuable addition to urban landscapes. Whether enhancing a building facade, producing food, or creating a green sanctuary, vertical gardens highlight the possibilities of integrating nature into modern architectural realms. By understanding the intricacies of these systems, farm owners and urban agriculturists can harness the full potential of vertical spaces.

CONTAINER GARDENING: FLEXIBILITY AND PORTABILITY

Container gardening refers to the cultivation of plants in any type of container rather than directly in the ground. The containers used can vary widely, from traditional pots to more innovative alternatives like old boots, wooden crates, or even hanging baskets.

Advantages of Container Gardening

Spatial Economy: Ideal for urban environments or places with limited garden space. Balconies, patios, and even indoor spaces can be transformed into green areas with container gardening.

Flexibility: Plants can be rearranged based on aesthetics or their sunlight requirements, providing dynamism to the space.

Controlled Environment: Soil quality, pH, and moisture can be managed effectively for each specific plant.

Portability: Seasonal changes or harsh weather conditions can be navigated by moving plants to more suitable locations.

Less Weeding: With a controlled soil environment, the chances of weed growth are minimized.

Choosing the Right Container

Material Considerations: Containers can be made of terracotta, wood, metal, ceramic, or plastic. Each has its advantages. Terracotta, for instance, is breathable but may dry out quickly. Plastic retains moisture but might not provide the same breathability.

Drainage: Essential for plant health. Ensure containers have adequate drainage holes.

Size and Depth: Must be chosen based on the plant's growth habits. Deep-rooted plants require deeper containers, while shallow ones suffice for most herbs and smaller plants.

Weight: If portability is a significant consideration, be mindful of the container's weight, especially when filled with soil and water.

The Importance of Quality Soil

Potting Mix: Specialized potting mixes available in the market are often more suitable for container gardening than regular garden soil. They offer good drainage and are generally lighter.

Soil-less Mixtures: Comprising coconut coir, perlite, and vermiculite, these mixes are lightweight, ensuring good aeration and moisture retention.

Fertilizer Integration: Since the nutrients in containers can be depleted faster, consider adding slow-release fertilizers or periodically feed with liquid fertilizers.

Watering Practices in Container Gardening

Monitoring: Containers tend to dry out faster. Regularly check the soil moisture.

Deep Watering: Ensure water reaches the roots. Surface watering may not suffice for deeper containers.

Overhead vs. Bottom Watering: While overhead watering is common, some plants, especially those susceptible to fungal diseases, might benefit from bottom watering.

Self-Watering Containers: These have a reservoir at the bottom, providing consistent moisture and reducing the frequency of watering.

Plant Selection for Containers

Size Growth Potential: While many plants can adapt to container life, be aware of their growth patterns. Large shrubs might not be suitable for small containers in the long run.

Edibles: Tomatoes, peppers, radishes, and various herbs thrive in containers. Consider dwarf or patio varieties of fruits for smaller spaces.

Ornamentals: Many flowering plants, from petunias to roses, can be grown in containers.

Trees: Dwarf tree varieties can be an impressive centerpiece in container gardening.

Container Garden Design Principles

Thriller, Filler, and Spiller: A popular design concept where the 'thriller' is a standout plant, the 'filler' occupies the middle space, and the 'spiller' cascades down the container.

Layering: For larger containers, creating layers with plants of varying heights can offer depth.

Color Coordination: Play with complementary or contrasting colors to create visually appealing arrangements.

Texture Play: Mix and match plants with different leaf textures or patterns for a more dynamic look.

Seasonal Considerations

Seasonal Swaps: Rotate plants based on the season. Spring bulbs can be replaced with summer blooms, followed by autumnal foliage.

Overwintering: In colder climates, some container plants might need protection or can be moved indoors to survive the winter.

Maintaining Container Health

Regular Pruning: Keep plants in shape and encourage fuller growth.

Rotation: Especially if sunlight is uneven, periodically rotate containers for uniform growth.

Pest and Disease Inspection: With closer proximity in container setups, pests or diseases can spread quickly. Regular checks and early interventions are essential.

Incorporating Technology

Drip Irrigation Systems: These can automate the watering process, especially useful for larger container gardens.

Smart Pots: Some modern containers come with built-in moisture and nutrient sensors, providing real-time feedback for better plant care.

Container gardening stands as a testament to the adaptability of nature. With the right knowledge and techniques, one can create thriving gardens in constrained spaces, proving that the essence of gardening is not bound by the expansiveness of land but by the passion and care of the gardener. In an increasingly urbanized world, container gardening becomes not just an aesthetic endeavor but also a means to bring nature closer to our everyday lives.

INTEGRATING VERTICAL AND CONTAINER GARDENING

Synergizing Vertical and Container Approaches

Vertical gardening and container gardening are not mutually exclusive concepts. When merged, they create a multi-dimensional space that maximizes productivity and aesthetic appeal while conserving space.

Dual Benefits

Space Utilization: Especially in urban environments with limited horizontal space, vertical container gardens can transform walls, balconies, and even windowsills into productive green spaces.

Microclimate Creation: When strategically placed, vertical container gardens can act as shields against harsh sunlight, windbreaks, or privacy screens, thus creating microclimates beneficial for other plants or for human comfort.

Structures for Vertical Container Gardens

Trellises and Lattices

These are frameworks of wood, metal, or plastic that provide support for climbing plants. They can be freestanding or affixed to walls. Containers can be hung or attached at intervals.

Vertical Pallet Gardens

Recycled wooden pallets can be modified to accommodate a multitude of small containers or a layered soil structure, making them suitable for herbs, succulents, or small flowering plants.

Green Walls and Modular Systems

Commercially available systems where containers or pockets are integrated into wall panels. These are particularly suitable for larger installations, both indoor and outdoor.

Tiered Planters

Stackable containers of descending size placed one atop the other, maximizing vertical space. This structure is ideal for herbs, strawberries, and smaller ornamental plants.

Plant Selection for Vertical Container Gardens

Weight Considerations

Given the vertical nature of the setup, it's vital to select plants that won't become too heavy when mature, which could strain or destabilize the supporting structure.

Growth Patterns

Plants with trailing or cascading growth habits, such as petunias or ivy, can be aesthetically pleasing in vertical setups. Conversely, plants with upward growth can be used for height variation.

Sunlight Requirements

When setting up a vertical container garden, consider the direction of sunlight. Place sun-loving plants at the top, where they can receive unobstructed light, while shade-loving plants can be placed lower down.

Soil and Nutrition in Vertical Container Systems

Given the non-traditional nature of vertical container setups, ensuring adequate nutrition for plants becomes crucial.

Lightweight Potting Mixes

Due to the vertical component, using a lighter potting mix, possibly with perlite or vermiculite, helps reduce overall weight without compromising on nutrient content.

Fertilization

Vertical gardens might necessitate more frequent fertilization than traditional gardens due to limited soil volume and quicker nutrient depletion. Employing slow-release granular fertilizers or periodic liquid feedings can counteract this.

Efficient Watering Techniques

Drip Irrigation Systems

By using a network of tubes, valves, and emitters, drip systems can provide a consistent and measured amount of water directly to the plant roots. This method is especially efficient for vertical setups, ensuring even water distribution across height.

Self-Watering Containers

Containers equipped with a reservoir can be beneficial in vertical gardening setups, especially in higher placements where manual watering might be challenging.

Regular Monitoring

Due to the vertical arrangement and potential for uneven water distribution, regular monitoring of soil moisture is essential to prevent both overwatering and underwatering.

Maintenance and Upkeep

Pruning and Training

For vertical growth, regular pruning can encourage more lateral and bushier growth, filling out the vertical space more effectively. Training plants, using ties or guides, can help direct growth and create a more organized appearance.

Pest and Disease Management

Given the closer proximity of plants in vertical container setups, it's essential to inspect regularly for pests or diseases and intervene promptly.

Structural Integrity Checks

Periodically assessing the strength and stability of vertical structures, especially after extreme weather events, ensures the safety and longevity of the garden.

Aesthetic Considerations

Color and Texture Variations

Combining plants with contrasting foliage colors or textures can create visually appealing patterns on a vertical plane. Think of the vertical space as a canvas, and use plants as the paint.

Seasonal Changes

Swapping out containers based on the season can keep the vertical garden looking fresh and vibrant throughout the year.

Economic Benefits and Sustainability

Reduced Land Costs

For commercial growers, vertical container gardens can drastically reduce the land required, leading to cost savings.

Sustainable Urban Farming

Vertical container gardens can play a pivotal role in urban agriculture, promoting local food production, reducing transportation emissions, and fostering a sense of community.

Rainwater Harvesting

Structures for vertical gardening can be integrated with rainwater harvesting systems, promoting water conservation.

While vertical and container gardening each bring their own set of advantages to the table, their integration amplifies their benefits manifold. Whether the goal is aesthetic enhancement, efficient land use, or sustainability, integrating vertical and container gardening offers solutions that are not just innovative but also deeply rooted in practicality. For modern farm owners, it provides an avenue to maximize production in limited spaces, fuse art with agriculture, and contribute to sustainable urban living.

CHALLENGES AND SOLUTIONS

Weight and Structural Support

Challenge: The vertical orientation of such gardens means that weight distribution is a primary concern. As plants mature, their weight, combined with that of the soil, water, and the containers themselves, can strain the structural integrity of the supporting framework.

Solution:

- **Initial Structural Assessment:** Before installing a vertical garden, a thorough evaluation of the intended structure or wall should be conducted. This ensures it can handle the load without compromising safety.
- **Use Lightweight Substrates:** Instead of traditional potting soil, consider lighter alternatives like coco coir, vermiculite, or hydroponic substrates.
- **Regular Maintenance:** Periodically trim plants to manage their weight and ensure healthy growth. Heavy plants should be placed at the bottom, while lighter ones can be positioned higher up.

Efficient Watering Mechanisms

Challenge: Ensuring even and adequate moisture to all plants, especially in a vertical arrangement, is challenging. There's a risk of waterlogging plants located at the bottom while leaving those at the top under-watered.

Solution:

- **Drip Irrigation Systems:** Such systems can be calibrated to deliver precise water quantities, ensuring all plants receive the moisture they need without wastage.
- **Self-Watering Containers:** These come equipped with water reservoirs, releasing moisture to plants as required.
- **Watering Timers:** These can be set to water plants at optimal times, like early morning or late evening, to reduce water evaporation and ensure maximum absorption.

Ensuring Uniform Light Distribution

Challenge: In vertical setups, plants may shade each other, leading to uneven light distribution, which can affect growth and yield.

Solution:

- **Strategic Plant Placement:** Position plants that require less light, such as ferns or certain herbs, below larger, sun-loving plants.

- **Supplemental Lighting:** In areas with inadequate natural light, consider installing LED grow lights. These can be placed at intervals to ensure that all plants receive the necessary light for photosynthesis.

Soil Compaction and Aeration

Challenge: Over time, the soil or substrate in containers can become compacted. This restricts root growth and reduces aeration, potentially stressing the plants.

Solution:

- **Regularly Loosen the Soil:** Every few weeks, gently aerate the soil using a fork or specialized tool. This ensures better air penetration to the roots.
- **Use Aerating Additives:** Perlite, vermiculite, or small pieces of pine bark can be mixed with the soil to improve aeration and prevent compaction.

Nutrient Management

Challenge: Plants in containers and vertical gardens may exhaust the nutrients in their limited soil volume faster than those in open ground.

Solution:

- **Regular Fertilization:** Use a balanced liquid fertilizer to regularly feed plants. The frequency will depend on the plants' growth stage and the substrate used.
- **Soil Testing:** Periodically test the soil or substrate for nutrient levels. This will provide insight into any deficiencies that need addressing.

Pest and Disease Management

Challenge: The close proximity of plants in vertical gardens can mean that pests and diseases spread quickly.

Solution:

- **Regular Monitoring:** Frequently inspect plants for signs of pests or diseases. Early detection is key to effective management.
- **Beneficial Insects:** Introduce beneficial insects, like ladybugs or lacewings, to manage pest populations naturally.
- **Isolate Affected Plants:** If a plant becomes infected, remove it promptly to prevent the spread of the disease to neighboring plants.

Root Space Limitation

Challenge: In vertical and container gardening, plants often have restricted root growth due to limited space.

Solution:

- **Choose Suitable Plants:** Opt for plants that naturally have a smaller root system or can thrive in confined spaces.

- **Regular Repotting:** Monitor root growth and repot plants when they outgrow their current containers.

Seasonal Adjustments

Challenge: Containers and vertical gardens can be sensitive to temperature changes. Soil in containers can heat up or cool down more rapidly than ground soil.

Solution:

- **Insulate Containers:** In colder months, insulate containers to protect roots from freezing. In hotter months, move containers to shadier locations or shield them from intense afternoon sun.

- **Adjust Watering:** Increase watering frequency during hotter periods and reduce during cooler, wetter times.

By addressing these challenges head-on and employing the outlined solutions, modern farm owners can optimize their vertical and container gardening endeavors, leading to healthy plants and maximized yields.

BENEFITS BEYOND SPACE SAVING

Enhanced Microclimate Control

Vertical gardens, especially when constructed on walls or structures, can influence the microclimate of the immediate surroundings. This not only benefits the plants but can also have positive implications for the nearby environment.

Temperature Regulation: Walls that have vertical gardens can experience reduced temperatures. This is primarily due to the cooling effect that results from the process of transpiration in plants. By acting as insulating layers, these gardens can stabilize indoor temperatures, potentially leading to energy savings.

Humidity Management: Vertical gardens can contribute to increased ambient humidity. Plants release water vapor into the atmosphere, helping in creating a moist microclimate.

This can be particularly beneficial in urban settings where concrete and asphalt typically result in dry conditions.

Air Quality Improvement

Plants are renowned for their ability to purify air. With vertical gardens, the density of plant growth in an area increases, amplifying this air-cleaning potential.

Pollutant Absorption: Many plants can absorb pollutants like formaldehyde, benzene, and nitrogen dioxide. With vertical gardens, the abundance of foliage can help reduce these harmful compounds, improving air quality.

Carbon Sequestration: Through photosynthesis, plants remove carbon dioxide from the atmosphere, releasing oxygen. The compact nature of vertical gardens ensures that significant amounts of CO_2 are converted, promoting cleaner air.

Noise Reduction

A less apparent yet valuable benefit of vertical gardens is their ability to dampen noise. This quality is especially valuable in urban or densely populated areas.

Sound Absorption: Plants, particularly their leaves, can act as sound absorbers. They can disrupt sound waves, reducing the volume of noise that passes through the garden.

Sound Insulation: If structured appropriately, vertical gardens can act as barriers that prevent the transmission of noise from one side to the other.

Biodiversity Boost

Despite their human-made nature, vertical gardens can become havens for various forms of life, playing a part in enhancing local biodiversity.

Attracting Beneficial Insects: Flowering plants can lure pollinators such as bees and butterflies. The presence of such beneficial insects can promote better fruiting and flowering in the garden and nearby areas.

Bird Habitats: Birds might also be attracted to vertical gardens for nesting or feeding on the insects present. This interaction helps in creating a balanced mini-ecosystem.

Mental and Physical Health Benefits

Gardens, regardless of their orientation, are known for the solace they provide. However, the unique structure of vertical gardens can amplify certain health benefits.

Psychological Wellbeing: The visual appeal of vertical gardens, combined with their dynamic nature (as plants grow and change), can act as stress-relievers. Engaging with these gardens, either through observation or maintenance, can have therapeutic effects.

Physiological Improvements: Plants release phytoncides, which are organic compounds that can bolster human immune responses. Additionally, the act of tending to a vertical garden can be a form of mild exercise, promoting physical health.

Enhanced Aesthetics and Real Estate Value

While functional benefits are primary, the aesthetic appeal of vertical gardens cannot be overlooked.

Architectural Enhancement: Vertical gardens can transform bland walls into living pieces of art. They can be designed to fit various architectural styles, adding a touch of nature to urban landscapes.

Property Value Boost: Incorporating vertical gardens can increase property value. They can make commercial and residential spaces more desirable, given their environmental and aesthetic contributions.

Water Conservation

Though it might seem counterintuitive, vertical gardens, when designed efficiently, can lead to water savings.

Efficient Irrigation: Drip irrigation systems in vertical gardens can ensure minimal water wastage. These systems deliver water directly to plant roots, reducing evaporation losses.

Water Recycling: Some vertical gardens are designed with water recirculation systems. Excess water at the bottom is collected and redirected to the top, ensuring optimal resource use.

Waste Reduction and Recycling

Vertical and container gardens provide unique opportunities for sustainable practices.

Composting: Organic waste can be composted and used as a nutrient-rich medium for plants. This practice reduces waste that would otherwise go to landfills.

Upcycling Containers: Old containers, which might be discarded, can be repurposed for gardening. This approach marries sustainability with creativity.

In sum, while vertical gardens and container gardening techniques are often pursued for their space-saving qualities, their benefits extend far beyond this. As modern farm owners, understanding and harnessing these multifaceted advantages can lead to more sustainable, beneficial, and efficient urban agricultural practices.

INCORPORATING TECHNOLOGY

Automated Drip Irrigation Systems

Efficient water use is paramount in vertical gardens. Overwatering can result in root rot, while insufficient water can quickly lead to plant stress due to the limited soil volume.

System Components: Automated drip systems often consist of a reservoir, pump, digital timer, and distribution tubes. These systems deliver water directly to the base of each plant, minimizing evaporation losses.

Sensor-based Adjustments: Advanced systems incorporate moisture sensors. These sensors assess the soil's moisture levels and activate the pump only when necessary, ensuring optimal water delivery and conservation.

LED Grow Lights

For indoor vertical gardens or those in areas with limited sunlight, artificial lighting becomes crucial. LED grow lights have emerged as the leading choice due to their energy efficiency and targeted light spectrum.

Spectrum Selection: Different plants have varied light needs. Some LEDs offer a full spectrum, while others can be adjusted to emit specific wavelengths conducive to vegetative growth or flowering.

Light Duration Control: Timers can be employed to control the duration of light exposure, ensuring plants get the right amount of "daylight" irrespective of external conditions.

Climate Control and Monitoring

Maintaining a stable environment is pivotal for plant health, especially in containerized settings.

Temperature and Humidity Sensors: These sensors continuously monitor environmental parameters. Data from these sensors can be accessed remotely via smartphones or computers.

Automated Environmental Adjustments: In conjunction with monitoring, systems can be designed to react to data. For instance, if humidity drops below a threshold, an automated mister could be activated.

Vertical Garden Management Software

Technology has facilitated the management of vertical gardens, especially on a commercial scale.

Garden Design and Planning: Software tools allow users to design their vertical garden layout, helping in determining plant placement, light positioning, and irrigation routing.

Maintenance Reminders: Such software can remind the gardener of tasks like pruning, fertilizing, or replacing growth mediums, ensuring no aspect of garden care is overlooked.

Vertical Farming Robotics

On a commercial scale, certain repetitive tasks have been entrusted to robots.

Robotic Plant Pruners: These robots can be programmed to prune plants, ensuring adequate air circulation and light penetration.

Harvesting Robots: Especially in large vertical farms, robots equipped with cameras and sensors can identify ripe produce and harvest them without causing damage.

Integrated Pest Management (IPM) Systems

Pests can be detrimental in a dense setting like vertical gardens. Technology assists in both monitoring and management.

Pest Detection Cameras: Cameras equipped with artificial intelligence can identify early signs of pest infestations, alerting the gardener to take action.

b. Automated Beneficial Insect Release: Some systems can release beneficial insects, like ladybugs, when harmful pests are detected, ensuring a biological control method.

Smart Pots and Containers

The very containers in which plants grow have seen technological enhancements.

Self-Watering Containers: These containers have built-in reservoirs that provide water to plants via wicking action, reducing the frequency of manual watering.

Root Monitoring Systems: Some smart pots come with sensors that monitor root health, alerting gardeners of potential issues like root-bound plants.

Data Analytics and Predictive Farming

Harnessing the power of data can lead to optimized yields and plant health.

Growth and Yield Analytics: By analyzing data from various sensors, gardeners can gain insights into factors that influence plant growth and make informed decisions.

Predictive Analysis: Advanced systems can forecast potential issues, like pest outbreaks or nutrient deficiencies, based on past data and trends.

Technology's embrace in the realm of vertical and container gardening underscores a broader shift towards precision agriculture. By integrating these technological tools, modern farm owners can ensure consistent yields, reduce resource waste, and address challenges proactively.

THE EMERGENCE OF GREENHOUSES IN MODERN AGRICULTURE

Greenhouses, enclosed structures designed to provide a controlled environment for plants, are quintessential for farm owners constrained by space or unsuitable outdoor climates. These structures effectively create a microclimate, enabling year-round cultivation of crops regardless of external weather conditions.

ANATOMY OF A GREENHOUSE

Delving into the modern greenhouse, we find an intricate blend of tradition and technology. These aren't just transparent structures letting in sunlight; they're precisely engineered environments to optimize plant growth. Let's traverse this fascinating world, peeling back the layers of what truly constitutes a greenhouse.

Structural Components

At the very heart of any greenhouse is its structure, a skeleton that holds everything together.

The Foundation: The silent sentinel, this component not only lends stability but also acts as a formidable barrier against pests and weeds. Whether it's concrete underfoot or treated wood, the foundation's primary job is to keep everything firmly rooted, especially in frost-prone regions where it needs to delve deep beneath the frost line.

The Frame: This is the backbone, gracefully arched in some greenhouses, angular in others, supporting the weight of the cladding and resisting the force of wind and snow. From the shimmering resilience of galvanized steel to the natural elegance of wood, the frame material and its design, like the Quonset or Gothic, are chosen based on aesthetic preferences and functionality.

End Walls: More than just the bookends of a greenhouse, these sturdy structures can be as transparent as the rest or provide shade with materials like polycarbonate panels. Besides housing the essential doors, vents, and fans, they're the guardians of airflow and temperature.

Cladding Materials

It's not just about letting in sunlight. The cladding, or the covering material, has an impressive role in light diffusion, heat retention, and weather protection.

Polyethylene: Ubiquitous and resilient, this UV-resistant covering offers commendable light diffusion. What's more, the economic viability ensures that its periodic replacement (typically every 3-5 years) doesn't break the bank.

Polycarbonate: The elite among cladding materials, its multi-wall structure does more than just shield plants. Those air pockets? They're nature's insulation, ensuring that the warmth stays in and the cold stays out.

Ventilation Systems

Every breath the greenhouse takes is orchestrated by its ventilation system, balancing temperature, replenishing essential carbon dioxide, and keeping humidity in check.

Natural Ventilation: Evoking the image of a greenhouse taking a deep breath, roof vents release the pent-up warm air, while the side vents welcome the cool breeze. The dance of vents, sometimes manual, sometimes automated, ensures a harmonious circulation.

Mechanical Ventilation: When nature needs a nudge, exhaust fans and intake louvers step in, creating a deliberate and directed flow of air, essential for those stifling peak-summer days.

Heating Systems

As winter unfurls, the greenhouse leans on its heating systems, ensuring that plants bask in optimal temperatures.

Forced Air Heaters: Like the comforting warmth of a fireplace, these heaters burn fuel and, with the aid of fans, spread warmth throughout, ensuring no plant feels left out in the cold.

Boiler Systems: Water, the eternal medium of life, carries warmth as it winds its way through pipes, sometimes embedded in the floor, sometimes on benches.

Cooling Systems

To beat the summer heat, greenhouses come equipped with their very own cooling systems.

Shade Systems: Whether draped inside or laid out externally, they act like sunglasses for plants, filtering out the intense rays of the sun.

Wet Wall Systems: Imagine the refreshing coolness of water cascading down a wall, evaporating and filling the space with a gentle chill. That's what a wet wall system brings to a greenhouse.

Benches and Flooring

Within these greenhouses, the arrangement is a symphony of space utilization and plant health.

Benches: From the sturdy permanence of fixed benches to the dynamic flexibility of rolling ones, they provide the stage for plants to flourish.

Flooring: Beyond being just the ground beneath, whether it's the solidity of concrete or the permeability of gravel, the flooring decides how water behaves – a critical aspect in preventing waterlogged roots.

Control Systems

The modern greenhouse isn't just brawn; there's a lot of brains involved. Advanced control systems are the nerve center, ensuring precision farming.

Thermostats and Hygrostats: Guardians of temperature and humidity, they spring into action, adjusting systems to maintain the ideal environment.

Computerized Control Systems: As we step into the future, greenhouses embrace technology. These systems offer a bird's-eye view of every aspect, from lighting to moisture levels, allowing for seamless integration and remote management.

This intricate anatomy of a greenhouse is an ode to the dedication of countless horticulturists and engineers. Each element, from the foundation to the control systems, plays a part in the symphony of growth, ensuring that each plant reaches its zenith in the safest and most nurturing environment.

OPERATIONAL DYNAMICS OF GREENHOUSES

Light Management

Greenhouses owe much of their effectiveness to their ability to harness and manipulate light. While sunlight provides a broad spectrum of light for plants, the operational dynamics involve intricate management to ensure every plant gets what it needs.

Light Diffusion: Not all sunlight is beneficial in its direct form. Through diffusing materials or screens, greenhouses can scatter sunlight, reducing shadow spots and ensuring a uniform exposure for all plants. This uniformity is paramount for consistent growth and maturity, especially in densely packed greenhouses.

Artificial Lighting: Seasons change, and with shorter days, supplementary lighting becomes essential. High-Intensity Discharge (HID) lights, LED lights, and fluorescents each have their niches in a greenhouse. Their implementation is based on plant needs, growth stages, and the desired photoperiod extension.

Light Duration Control: Certain plants require specific photoperiods to flower or fruit. By controlling the duration of light exposure, greenhouses can induce flowering or extend vegetative growth as needed.

Temperature Regulation Techniques

Temperature plays a decisive role in plant metabolism, growth rate, and overall health. Operational dynamics in greenhouses revolve around maintaining this temperature within optimal ranges.

Shade Systems: Beyond their role in cooling, shades play a pivotal role in regulating temperature. Retractable shade systems, either manual or automated, give greenhouses the flexibility to adapt to changing external conditions.

Thermal Screens: These are specially designed materials that trap heat. Deployed during colder nights, they act as insulation, minimizing heat loss and stabilizing internal temperatures.

Ground and Air Heating: From radiant heat systems embedded in the floor to overhead heaters, maintaining the right temperature is a symphony of circulation fans, heaters, and sensors working in tandem.

Water and Irrigation Management

A plant's relationship with water in a greenhouse is a delicate balance. Too much or too little can be detrimental, making water management a core operational dynamic.

Drip Irrigation: Delivering water directly to the base of plants minimizes waste and ensures a uniform supply. This localized application also helps in reducing the spread of waterborne diseases.

Misting and Fogging: Used primarily for humidity control, these systems can also provide cooling during hot periods. They break water into fine droplets, ensuring rapid evaporation and effective humidity control.

Water Collection and Recycling: Modern greenhouses employ systems that collect excess water, filter it, and then reintroduce it into the irrigation system. This sustainable approach conserves water and ensures that nutrients are not wasted.

Carbon Dioxide Enrichment

For plants, carbon dioxide (CO_2) is as vital as oxygen is for humans. Enhancing CO_2 levels can dramatically increase plant growth and productivity.

CO_2 Generators: By burning propane or natural gas, these generators produce CO_2 which is then circulated within the greenhouse.

Liquid CO2 Systems: Deployed in larger commercial setups, these systems release CO2 from stored liquid sources, ensuring precise control over ambient levels.

Monitoring and Automation: Constant monitoring of CO2 levels is essential. Too much or too little can impact plant health. Automated systems ensure levels are consistently maintained within the desired range.

Pest and Disease Management

A contained environment can be a double-edged sword. While it offers protection from many external threats, if pests or diseases gain a foothold, they can proliferate rapidly.

Integrated Pest Management (IPM): This holistic approach involves introducing beneficial insects, practicing crop rotation, and employing bio-pesticides to manage pest populations.

Quarantine and Inspection: Regular checks, especially of new plant introductions, can prevent infestations. Quarantine areas in greenhouses ensure that any potential threat is neutralized before it can spread.

UV Sterilization: Used primarily for water sources, UV systems kill pathogens, ensuring that the water used for irrigation is free from potential disease vectors.

Digital Monitoring and Automation

The contemporary greenhouse is a blend of nature and technology.

Sensory Networks: From soil moisture sensors to ambient light detectors, a network of sensors constantly feeds data into central systems, ensuring conditions remain optimal.

Remote Management: With the rise of IoT (Internet of Things), greenhouse operations can be monitored and controlled remotely. This capability allows for immediate interventions, even if the operator isn't physically present.

Predictive Analysis: Leveraging data analytics, modern greenhouses can forecast issues before they become critical. Whether it's a potential pest outbreak or an impending nutrient deficiency, predictive systems offer a proactive approach to management.

The operational dynamics of a greenhouse are a testament to human ingenuity and the drive to mimic and enhance nature's processes. Every component, every system works in harmony, creating a controlled Eden where plants can thrive, shielded from external vagaries, yet basking in an environment that is as close to nature's ideal as humanly possible.

BENEFITS OF GREENHOUSE CULTIVATION

In the transformative journey of modern agriculture, greenhouses stand out as monumental game-changers. Their advent has unlocked an array of benefits that extend beyond the obvious advantage of space optimization.

Extended Growing Season and its Economic Repercussions

The controlled environment inside a greenhouse is a boon to cultivators, offering a haven from the unpredictable elements of nature. Instead of being bound by seasonal changes, farmers can now cultivate throughout the year. This consistent production cycle doesn't merely translate to increased produce, but also to steadier revenue streams. The ability to simulate the best conditions for plant growth ensures that crops can mature faster, paving the way for quicker turnovers and enhanced yields within confined timelines.

Efficient Resource Utilization: The Pinnacle of Sustainable Farming

Greenhouses champion the cause of sustainable farming. Precision irrigation systems, such as drip and fogger setups, significantly curtail water usage when compared to their traditional counterparts. When you add rainwater harvesting and recycling to this mix, the water efficiency of greenhouses reaches commendable levels.

Moreover, with techniques like high-density planting and vertical farming, greenhouses champion productivity, producing an abundance on relatively small patches of land. The precision offered by fertigation systems not only curtails nutrient wastage but also ensures that plants get a perfectly balanced diet for optimal growth.

Enhancing Crop Protection and Quality

Greenhouses act as a protective shield, safeguarding crops from harsh weather conditions, from torrid suns to torrential downpours. This protection is invaluable in regions prone to unpredictable weather patterns or extreme conditions.

Moreover, the enclosed nature of greenhouses offers an added layer of protection against pests and diseases. This controlled environment significantly reduces the spread of these threats. The direct result? Crops that not only look better but also taste superior, thanks to their consistent growth conditions and minimal exposure to harmful agents.

Flexibility and the Joy of Diversification

For a farmer, the joy of cultivating non-native crops or experimenting with exotic varieties is unmatched. Greenhouses make this possible. Whether it's a tropical fruit in a temperate zone or an exotic flower that usually wilts in the local climate, greenhouses break down geographical barriers.

Furthermore, with the capability to create specific conditions, greenhouses have given rise to the cultivation of gourmet crops, offering products that fetch premium prices in the market, adding a lucrative dimension to farming.

Sustainability and Environmental Stewardship

Greenhouses are harbingers of eco-friendly farming. Especially those powered by renewable energy sources. Advanced greenhouses even integrate mechanisms to capture and reuse CO_2. Add to this the prevention of soil degradation through soilless farming methods and the reduced reliance on chemical agents, and you have a farming method that's as clean as it's efficient.

Harnessing the Power of Technology

In the age of digitization, greenhouses seamlessly blend traditional farming with modern technology. Data-driven decisions have become the norm, with sensors offering insights into every aspect of the farming process, from soil moisture levels to ambient temperature. This abundance of data, coupled with automation, ensures a level of consistency and efficiency previously deemed unattainable.

Furthermore, the controlled nature of greenhouses makes them perfect for agricultural research and development. It's here that the future of farming is shaped, with new crop varieties and innovative techniques being put to the test.

In the vast panorama of agriculture, greenhouses shine brightly. They represent a confluence of tradition and innovation, offering a glimpse into the future of farming—a future that promises abundance, quality, and sustainability.

TRANSITION TO HYDROPONICS WITHIN GREENHOUSES

Hydroponics, the method of cultivating plants without soil, instead using nutrient-rich water solutions, is an innovation that pairs seamlessly with greenhouse cultivation.

ADVANTAGES OF HYDROPONIC CULTIVATION

The Interplay of Soil-less Farming and Controlled Environments

The future of agriculture, in many ways, is moving away from the traditional to embrace modern, innovative techniques. At the forefront of this shift is hydroponic cultivation—a system that eschews soil in favor of nutrient-rich water solutions to sustain plant growth. When integrated within the confines of greenhouses, hydroponics takes on a new dimension, amalgamating the advantages of both systems.

Precision in Nutrient Delivery

At the very essence of hydroponics is the direct and precise delivery of nutrients to plant roots. In traditional soil-based farming, the roots need to search for their required nutrients, often facing inconsistent or inadequate supplies. In hydroponic systems, however, a balanced nutrient solution surrounds the roots, ensuring that plants receive exactly what they need, when they need it. This precision leads to faster growth rates, higher yields, and, frequently, enhanced quality of produce.

Efficient Water Use and Conservation

A salient feature of hydroponics is its water efficiency. While traditional farming methods can lead to significant water wastage due to evaporation, runoff, and inefficient absorption, hydroponic systems recirculate water. This ensures that plants take up the majority of the water supplied, with minimal loss. The implications of this efficiency are vast, especially in regions where water is a scarce resource.

Space Optimization and Increased Crop Density

Hydroponic systems, by their very design, allow for a more efficient use of space. Since there's no need for extensive root growth to search for nutrients (as the nutrients are directly available), plants can be placed much closer together. This increased crop density means that more plants can be cultivated in the same area compared to traditional farming—a boon for greenhouses where space is at a premium.

Reduction in Pests and Diseases

Soil is often a reservoir for various pests and diseases. By eliminating soil from the equation, hydroponics significantly reduces the chances of soil-borne diseases. While hydroponic systems are not entirely immune to pests and diseases, the controlled environment of a greenhouse, combined with the cleanliness of hydroponic systems, drastically reduces the risks.

Flexibility in Crop Rotation

One of the lesser-celebrated advantages of hydroponics is the flexibility it offers in terms of crop rotation. In traditional farming, the soil's health and nutrient levels can dictate what crops can be planted in succession. With hydroponics, since the nutrient solution can be adjusted as needed, farmers have greater flexibility in determining crop sequences, ensuring optimal yields throughout the year.

Lower Reliance on Herbicides and Pesticides

The very nature of hydroponic cultivation—being predominantly indoors and devoid of soil—means that many common agricultural pests are naturally excluded. As a result, there's a significant reduction in the need for chemical interventions in the form of herbicides and pesticides. This not only translates to cleaner produce but also reduces the environmental impact of farming operations.

Scalability and Modularity

Hydroponic systems within greenhouses are inherently modular. Whether you're starting with a single table or an entire greenhouse section dedicated to hydroponics, the system can be expanded relatively easily. This modularity ensures that as demand grows or as the farm owner becomes more proficient in hydroponic techniques, the system can scale accordingly.

Enhanced Produce Quality and Consistency

The controlled nature of hydroponic cultivation often results in produce of superior quality. Given the precise nutrient delivery and optimal growing conditions, fruits, vegetables, and herbs grown hydroponically often exhibit richer flavors, brighter colors, and better textures. Moreover, the consistency achieved in hydroponic systems is unparalleled, ensuring that consumers receive the same quality of produce batch after batch.

COMMON HYDROPONIC SYSTEMS FOR GREENHOUSE INTEGRATION

When contemplating the integration of hydroponic systems within greenhouses, one must delve deep into the intricacies of each system to understand how they function in symbiosis with the controlled environment of a greenhouse. A seamless integration ensures not just the survival but the thriving of crops in an optimized environment. Let's explore the various systems in detail.

Nutrient Film Technique (NFT)

The Nutrient Film Technique often simply referred to as NFT, stands out due to its uniqueness in design and efficiency. At its core, NFT is a water-saving marvel. It relies on a continuous but shallow stream of nutrient solution that glides over the plant roots. This 'film' of nutrient solution is what gives the system its name.

Design Essentials: A quintessential NFT system is built using channels or troughs, usually crafted from PVC or other inert materials. These channels are strategically placed at a slight angle, ensuring the gravitational movement of the nutrient solution.

Root Dynamics in NFT: Plant roots in NFT systems are partially submerged in the nutrient film, with the upper part of the roots exposed to the humid air. This ensures that the roots receive both nutrients from the water and oxygen from the air. One might wonder about the absence of a traditional growing medium. NFT dispenses with this need, using only net pots or similar structures to anchor the plants and provide initial support.

Greenhouse Symbiosis: Pairing an NFT system with a greenhouse is, in many ways, a match made in agricultural heaven. The controlled environment of the greenhouse provides the stability required for the nutrient solution, ensuring it remains at an optimum temperature. Moreover, being in a shielded space means there's a reduced risk of external contaminants affecting the nutrient solution.

Deep Water Culture (DWC)

If one were to consider hydroponics in its most straightforward form, Deep Water Culture, or DWC, would be a prime example. Simplicity, however, doesn't detract from its effectiveness.

The Essence of DWC: Visualize a reservoir filled with a nutrient-rich solution. Above this reservoir, plants are suspended, their roots immersing deeply into the nutrient bath. It's a direct, effective system, but there's one challenge it must overcome: oxygenation. This is where air stones or diffusers come into play, releasing a stream of air bubbles to ensure the solution remains oxygen-rich.

Sustaining Plant Growth: The continuous access to nutrients and the oxygen-rich environment promote rapid plant growth. Plant roots are in their element, absorbing everything they need without any hindrance.

The Greenhouse Advantage: Marrying DWC with greenhouse cultivation creates an optimal ecosystem for the plants. The consistent environment within the greenhouse ensures that there's minimal stress on the plants, allowing them to focus solely on growth. The protection from external pests and diseases is an added boon.

Ebb and Flow (Flood and Drain)

Drawing inspiration from nature's tidal systems, the Ebb and Flow method has carved a niche for itself in the hydroponic community.

Understanding the Mechanism: Central to this system is the intermittent flooding and draining of the plant roots. Plants sit comfortably in a tray, and at set intervals, this tray experiences a 'high tide', where it's flooded with nutrient solution. Post this, a 'low tide' phase ensues, draining the solution and allowing the roots a breather.

Components in Play: The reservoir, containing the nutrient solution, is the heart of the system. The grow tray, a pump to manage the ebb and flow, and timers to regulate the process complete the ensemble.

In a Greenhouse Setting: When this system finds a home within a greenhouse, it thrives. The ambient conditions within the greenhouse, such as consistent temperature and humidity levels, make it easier to regulate the flooding cycles, optimizing nutrient uptake and minimizing water loss.

Drip Systems

Precision and efficiency are the cornerstones of drip hydroponic systems.

Underlying Principle: From a main reservoir, a network of tubes fan out, culminating in drip emitters positioned close to each plant's base. The nutrient solution is thus delivered directly to where it's needed most, ensuring maximum uptake.

Controlling the Flow: Drip emitters are more than mere endpoints; they're gatekeepers. They can be adjusted to release specific volumes of the solution, giving farmers unparalleled control over nutrient distribution.

Greenhouse Synergy: Using drip systems in greenhouses conserves both water and nutrients, thanks to reduced evaporation. The controlled environment ensures that each plant receives its fair share of nutrients, leading to uniform and healthy growth across the board.

Aeroponics

On the cutting edge of hydroponic innovation, aeroponics pushes the boundaries of what's possible in soilless cultivation.

Roots in the Air: Unlike traditional systems, aeroponics sees plants suspended with their roots in open air. Periodically, these dangling roots are misted with a nutrient-rich solution, keeping them moist and nourished.

The Setup: Within a chamber, plants are held in position using foam inserts or similar structures. This chamber houses misters or nozzles that intermittently spray the roots, ensuring they remain in prime condition.

A Greenhouse Home: An aeroponic system and a greenhouse are complementary forces. The controlled conditions within a greenhouse, such as high humidity levels, ensure roots retain optimum moisture. The stable temperatures further allow for a precise misting regimen, ensuring plants receive consistent nourishment.

The world of hydroponics offers a plethora of systems, each with its unique set of advantages. When these systems find a partner in greenhouses, they create an environment where plants not only grow but flourish. By understanding the intricacies of each system and aligning them with the controlled environment of a greenhouse, we can pave the way for sustainable, efficient, and productive farming practices.

MAINTENANCE AND MONITORING IN HYDROPONIC GREENHOUSES

Nutrient Solution Management

The lifeblood of any hydroponic system is its nutrient solution. This mixture of water and essential minerals sustains plant life in the absence of soil, ensuring they receive all necessary nutrients.

pH Level Checks: Maintaining the optimal pH level ensures maximum nutrient uptake by plants. Regular checks, preferably daily, are crucial. Most plants thrive in a pH range of 5.5 to 6.5, but specific crops might have individual preferences. Adjusting the pH can be achieved using pH up or down solutions.

Electrical Conductivity (EC) Measurements: EC provides a snapshot of the nutrient concentration within the solution. Over time, as plants absorb nutrients, the EC will decrease. Monitoring ensures the solution remains potent and can inform when it's time to replenish or replace the mixture.

Periodic Solution Replacement: Over time, nutrient imbalances can occur due to selective uptake by plants. Periodically refreshing the solution, usually every 1-2 weeks, ensures consistent nutrition.

System Cleanliness and Sterilization

In the closed environment of a hydroponic greenhouse, cleanliness isn't just about aesthetics; it's a bulwark against disease and contamination.

Root Health Inspection: Regular visual checks of plant roots can pre-empt many issues. Healthy roots typically appear white or pale, while brown, slimy roots can indicate root rot or other diseases.

System Flushing: Periodic flushing of the entire system with clean water can rid it of any nutrient buildup, preventing potential blockages or imbalances.

Sterilization: Between crop cycles, it's advisable to sterilize the entire setup using hydrogen peroxide or other commercial hydroponic system cleaners. This ensures any lingering pathogens are eradicated.

Climate Control and Monitoring

The symbiotic relationship between hydroponics and greenhouses is underscored by climate control. Precise environmental conditions can lead to maximized yields.

Temperature Regulation: Each plant species has its ideal temperature range. Advanced greenhouses are equipped with automated HVAC systems that maintain this optimal range, accommodating the requirements of the hydroponic system and the crops inside.

Humidity Levels: Especially crucial in aeroponics or NFT systems, maintaining the right humidity ensures roots receive adequate moisture from the air. Dehumidifiers or humidifiers, depending on the climate, can be employed to maintain desired levels.

CO2 Management: Enhanced CO_2 levels can stimulate plant growth. By monitoring and adjusting the CO_2 concentration within the greenhouse, growers can provide an additional boost to their crops.

Pest and Disease Vigilance

The absence of soil doesn't make hydroponic systems immune to pests or diseases, but it does alter the dynamics.

Regular Visual Checks: Routine inspections can catch infestations early. Look for telltale signs on leaves, stems, and even the nutrient solution's surface.

Biological Control: Rather than resorting to chemicals, many hydroponic greenhouse operators use beneficial insects to counter pests. Ladybugs, for example, are natural predators of aphids.

Systemic Solutions: In case of a disease outbreak, systemic solutions that plants absorb can help combat the issue from within.

Hardware and Infrastructure Checks

The mechanical and structural components of a hydroponic system require regular maintenance to ensure longevity and efficient operation.

Pump and Reservoir Maintenance: The heart of many hydroponic systems, pumps must be inspected for signs of wear, tear, or blockages. The reservoir should be cleaned during each solution change to prevent algae buildup.

Drip Emitter and Nozzle Checks: For systems using drip or misting methods, the small components can become clogged. Regular checks and cleaning can prevent disruptions.

Support and Anchoring Systems: The physical support—be it trellises, net pots, or other anchoring systems—should be inspected for stability, ensuring plants remain secure as they grow.

Data Collection and Analysis

Modern hydroponic greenhouses are often data-driven operations. Harnessing technology for monitoring can lead to optimized yields.

Digital pH and EC Meters: Moving beyond manual tests, digital meters offer real-time insights into the nutrient solution's condition, with some systems even allowing remote monitoring.

Climate Control Systems: Sophisticated systems now offer integrative solutions, allowing growers to set desired conditions and receive alerts if parameters drift out of range.

Growth and Yield Metrics: By meticulously recording growth rates, flowering times, and yield quantities, growers can refine their methods over time, tweaking variables for optimal results.

In the nexus of hydroponics and greenhouses, maintenance and monitoring are the twin pillars upon which success rests. By diligently tending to both the living components—plants, nutrient solutions—and the mechanical ones, a harmonious balance can be achieved. This ensures not only the health of the crops but the sustainability and efficiency of the system as a whole.

CHALLENGES IN GREENHOUSE HYDROPONICS AND MITIGATION STRATEGIES

Nutrient Management Challenges

Nutrient Imbalances: Within hydroponic systems, maintaining a perfect balance of nutrients is crucial. Over time, plants may absorb certain nutrients more than others, leading to imbalances that can affect plant health and yield.

Mitigation: Periodic testing and adjusting of the nutrient solution is key. This can be done through the use of digital EC and pH meters, which provide real-time data on nutrient concentrations, enabling timely adjustments.

Salt Buildup: Certain nutrients, when left unchecked, can accumulate and form salts that could harm plant roots, impeding their ability to absorb water and essential nutrients.

Mitigation: Flushing the system periodically with fresh water can prevent salt accumulation. Using reverse osmosis water can also minimize the risk of salt buildup.

Disease and Pest Management

Root Rot: In hydroponic systems, especially those where roots are continuously submerged, there's a risk of root rot. This fungal disease can spread rapidly and is detrimental to plant health.

Mitigation: Proper aeration of the nutrient solution and ensuring the solution's cleanliness can prevent root rot. Also, beneficial microbes can be introduced to outcompete the harmful fungi.

Pest Infestation: While hydroponics does reduce soil-borne pests, it doesn't eliminate the risk entirely. Aphids, spider mites, and whiteflies, among others, can still pose challenges.

Mitigation: Regular inspections, use of organic insecticides, and introduction of natural predators can keep pest populations in check. Ensure the greenhouse is sealed properly to prevent entry.

Technical Challenges

System Failures: Pumps, timers, and other mechanical components can fail, interrupting the nutrient flow and jeopardizing plant health.

Mitigation: Regular equipment checks, having backup systems in place, and promptly replacing worn-out parts can prevent prolonged downtimes.

Calibration Issues: Instruments like pH and EC meters require regular calibration to remain accurate. Neglect can lead to incorrect readings and consequent poor decision-making.

Mitigation: Adhere to a strict schedule for instrument calibration using standard solutions. Investing in quality instruments that hold their calibration longer is also advisable.

Environmental Control Challenges

Temperature Fluctuations: Consistent temperature is vital for plant growth. Fluctuations can stress plants, reducing yield quality and quantity.

Mitigation: Modern greenhouses can be equipped with automated HVAC systems that monitor and adjust temperatures in real-time. Insulating materials can also stabilize internal temperatures.

Humidity Imbalances: Excess humidity can promote mold growth, while too little can stress plants. Achieving the right balance is essential.

Mitigation: Automated dehumidifiers and humidifiers, paired with sensors, can maintain the desired humidity levels. Proper ventilation can also aid in regulating humidity.

Hydroponic greenhouse farming, while promising in its potential, comes with its set of challenges. However, with proper knowledge, strategies, and a proactive approach, these challenges can be mitigated, paving the way for a successful and productive farming endeavor.

INCORPORATING TECHNOLOGY IN GREENHOUSE HYDROPONICS

In the realm of greenhouse cultivation, hydroponics emerges as a beacon of modernity. Not only does this method challenge traditional soil-based practices, but it also redefines how we perceive plant growth, health, and productivity. Yet, at the heart of this revolution lies an even more profound transformation: the confluence of hydroponics with technology.

The Precision of Automated Nutrient Delivery

In the intricate ballet of plant growth, nutrients play a pivotal role. As any seasoned farmer would acknowledge, the delicate balance between various minerals and salts can profoundly influence the health and yield of crops. Previously, managing this equilibrium was an exercise that leaned heavily on human expertise and diligence. Today, however, technology ensures this balance is maintained with precision.

Advanced nutrient dosing systems have become invaluable assets in the hydroponic space. With sensors diligently tracking nutrient concentrations, these systems calibrate the nutrient mix, ensuring plants receive the exact nutrition they need. This automation eliminates guesswork, dramatically reduces human error, and ensures that plants consistently access the optimal nutrient blend, leading to healthier crops and better yields.

Environmental Mastery with Climate Control

If nutrient management was one part of the equation, ensuring the perfect environmental conditions within the greenhouse represents the other half. With climate control systems, the environment isn't left to chance or external climatic whims.

Modern systems continuously monitor and adjust a range of parameters, including temperature, humidity, CO_2 levels, and light. The level of control that technology offers means that even if there's a heatwave outside, the lettuce crops inside the greenhouse remain cool, crisp, and in prime condition.

Data-Driven Farming: From Insights to Actions

One cannot emphasize enough the value of data in modern greenhouse hydroponics. It's not just about collecting numbers; it's about translating these numbers into actionable insights. Wireless sensors, scattered across the greenhouse, paint a real-time picture of the environment, nutrient levels, and even plant health.

The aggregation of this data, when processed through sophisticated software platforms, offers insights that were previously impossible to glean. For instance, tracking growth patterns over time can help identify optimal conditions for specific crop phases or even predict when a plant is likely to face stress.

The AI Revolution in Hydroponics

While data analysis provides the present's clarity, artificial intelligence offers a glimpse into the future. By studying past patterns and current conditions, AI algorithms can forecast future challenges or opportunities. Whether it's predicting a pest infestation before it manifests or adjusting nutrient dosages to preempt plant stress, AI has started playing an invaluable role in proactive farm management.

LED Lighting: More Than Just Illumination

Light, as we know, is vital for plant growth. Yet, technology has transformed this basic element into a tool of precision agriculture. Modern LED systems used in greenhouses can be fine-tuned to emit specific light spectrums, influencing plant growth, flowering, and even nutritional content. It's no longer about merely illuminating the greenhouse; it's about curating light to achieve desired outcomes.

Monitoring and Responsive Systems

Beyond just collecting data, modern greenhouses are becoming increasingly responsive. For instance, if a sensor detects a sudden drop in humidity levels, automated systems can immediately adjust misting or ventilation systems to correct the anomaly. This seamless interaction between sensors and actuators ensures the environment remains consistently conducive for plant growth, regardless of external challenges.

Interconnectivity and Remote Management

In today's interconnected world, greenhouse management isn't confined to those physically present on the farm. Advanced hydroponic systems often come equipped with remote management capabilities. This means that a farmer, equipped with a smartphone or laptop, can monitor, adjust, and control various greenhouse parameters from virtually anywhere in the world.

Technology's integration into hydroponic greenhouses isn't merely about enhancing efficiency or reducing labor costs. It's about redefining what's possible. It's about merging the time-tested wisdom of traditional farming with the precision of modern science. As technology continues to evolve, one can only imagine the boundaries that greenhouse hydroponics will push in the years to come.

ECONOMIC CONSIDERATIONS IN GREENHOUSE HYDROPONICS

Capital Expenditure in Infrastructure

Transitioning to greenhouse hydroponics typically involves significant initial capital expenditure. Beyond the greenhouse structure itself, the choice of hydroponic systems—whether it's nutrient film technique, deep water culture, aeroponics, or a hybrid approach—determines the foundational investment. It's crucial to select materials and systems that match the intended scale of operation, ensuring they provide value for money.

Land Optimization and Value

Greenhouse hydroponics allows farmers to achieve higher yields per square foot compared to traditional farming. Though the initial investment might seem steep, the returns per unit area can justify the costs. With land prices escalating in many regions, optimizing land use becomes a critical economic factor. Greenhouse hydroponics offers the ability to cultivate on terrains that may not be naturally fertile or conducive to traditional farming.

Operational Expenditure and Recurring Costs

Once set up, the day-to-day running costs of a hydroponic greenhouse become the focus. From the purchase of nutrient solutions and growth mediums to energy costs, the recurring expenditure is ongoing.

- **Nutrient Solutions:** Tailored nutrient solutions are vital for plant growth in hydroponics. The cost of these solutions and their management, including pH balance and nutrient concentration, impacts operational costs.

- **Water and Filtration:** While hydroponic systems typically use less water than traditional farming, there are costs associated with obtaining high-quality water, and in some cases, water treatment or filtration systems are necessary.

- **Labor Costs:** Hydroponics may reduce some manual tasks such as weeding, but it demands a different skill set. Hiring or training staff to manage the systems, understand plant nutrition, and tackle potential problems is a factor to consider.

Economic Benefits from Crop Turnover

One of the significant advantages of greenhouse hydroponics is the possibility of multiple crop turnovers in a year. Controlled conditions allow for year-round cultivation, irrespective of external weather patterns. This can lead to higher annual yields and thus more consistent revenue streams.

Diversification and Premium Produce

Growing in a controlled environment allows farmers to diversify their produce. They can venture into exotic crops that fetch a premium price in the market. Additionally, hydroponic produce, often deemed cleaner due to the lack of soil and reduced pesticide use, can command a higher market value.

Cost Efficiency and Sustainability: Interlinked Concepts

Efficient systems can lead to sustainability, both environmentally and economically. Investing in renewable energy sources for powering greenhouses can reduce long-term energy costs. Solar panels, for instance, might have an upfront cost but can offer substantial savings over time.

Waste Management and Recycling

In hydroponics, the efficient use of resources is both an economic and environmental advantage. Recycling water within the system can lead to savings. Similarly, the reuse or composting of spent growth mediums can reduce costs associated with waste disposal and purchasing new materials.

Scalability and Expansion

For farm owners looking to the future, the modular nature of many hydroponic systems means they can scale their operations as demand grows. This scalability can spread out costs, ensuring that expansion doesn't always mean a linear rise in expenditure.

Risk Management: Preparing for Uncertainties

Every agricultural venture has inherent risks, and hydroponics is no exception. Equipment malfunctions, disease outbreaks, or market fluctuations can affect profitability. It's crucial to set aside contingency funds and perhaps even consider insurance options tailored for hydroponic farming.

Market Research and Trends

Staying attuned to market demands and trends is vital. While certain crops might fetch a premium today, market saturation or changing consumer preferences can shift the landscape. Regularly updating market research can help farm owners pivot their crop choices or marketing strategies, ensuring they maximize their revenue potential.

The transition to hydroponics within greenhouses, while representing a substantial financial commitment, offers a plethora of economic benefits in the long run. Proper planning, understanding the recurring costs, and being agile in response to market demands can set the stage for a profitable venture in this modern farming frontier.

COMMUNITY AND ENVIRONMENTAL IMPACT

Enhancing Local Food Security

One of the cardinal implications of adopting hydroponic systems within greenhouses is the contribution to local food security. By utilizing controlled environments, crops can be grown year-round, independent of seasonal restrictions, and often at higher yields than traditional methods. This consistent supply aids in stabilizing local food sources, reducing dependency on imported goods, and providing communities with fresh, local produce.

Job Creation and Skill Development

With the transition to these high-tech farming methods, new roles emerge within the agricultural sector. While some might fear a reduction in traditional farming jobs, the reality is more of a shift than a reduction. Hydroponic greenhouse systems require personnel trained in system management, plant nutrition, and technological interfacing. As farms adopt these systems, opportunities for training and upskilling local individuals arise, fostering skill development and generating employment.

Water Conservation and Management

Hydroponic systems, by design, use water more efficiently than soil-based cultivation. This efficiency is a boon in regions facing water scarcity. By recycling and reusing water within closed-loop systems, hydroponic greenhouses dramatically reduce water wastage. The implications are two-fold: firstly, it ensures that farming remains viable even in water-stressed regions; secondly, it alleviates pressure on local water resources, benefiting the broader community and ecosystem.

Reduced Land Degradation and Soil Erosion

Traditional farming, especially when improperly managed, can lead to land degradation and soil erosion. By shifting to hydroponics, the reliance on soil as a growth medium is eliminated. This shift has positive repercussions for the environment, preserving land quality and preventing detrimental runoff that can pollute waterways.

Carbon Footprint and Transport Implications

A localized approach to agriculture, facilitated by hydroponic greenhouses, can significantly reduce the carbon footprint associated with transporting produce. When communities source their food locally rather than from distant locations, the emissions from transportation diminish. This not only aids in reducing the overall environmental impact but also ensures that produce is fresher and retains more nutritional value by the time it reaches consumers.

Pesticide Reduction and Ecosystem Health

Greenhouse hydroponics offers a controlled environment, reducing the incidence of pests and diseases. As a result, the reliance on chemical pesticides can be substantially lowered. This reduction benefits both the environment and consumers. Fewer chemicals mean healthier ecosystems, with positive implications for local biodiversity. Consumers, in turn, receive produce that has a lower chemical residue, aligning with the increasing demand for organic and cleanly-grown food.

Urban Farming and Community Cohesion

The adaptability of hydroponic systems means they are not restricted to rural settings. Urban and peri-urban environments can host greenhouse hydroponics, bringing farming into cities. This urban integration promotes community cohesion, offering city-dwellers a connection to their food sources and fostering understanding and appreciation for agriculture. Urban farms can become community hubs, places of learning, and centers for social interaction.

Waste Management and Resource Efficiency

In hydroponic systems, resource efficiency is heightened. The ability to recycle nutrients and water means less wastage. Moreover, the absence of soil eliminates soil-based waste. For communities, this efficient resource use can translate to reduced pressure on waste management systems and a smaller environmental footprint.

Promotion of Sustainable Practices

The very nature of hydroponics within greenhouses promotes sustainable agricultural practices. By controlling inputs and environments, waste is minimized, and yields are maximized. The broader community stands to benefit from these sustainable practices, enjoying a consistent supply of fresh produce with a smaller carbon footprint. Moreover, as community members witness the benefits of sustainable farming, it might encourage the adoption of sustainable practices in other areas of life.

Economic Implications for the Community

Beyond the direct economic benefits to the farm owner, the community stands to gain economically from the transition to hydroponic greenhouses. Local produce can often fetch premium prices, especially if branded as sustainably grown or organic. This premium not only boosts local economies but can also lead to agritourism opportunities, where interested individuals visit farms to learn about hydroponic techniques.

In essence, the transition to hydroponics within greenhouses has far-reaching implications, both for the immediate community and the environment at large. The benefits are multifaceted, from economic gains and job creation to environmental preservation and enhanced food security. As modern farm owners, recognizing and harnessing these advantages is not just a route to business success but a step towards a sustainable and community-centric future.

SOWING ESSENTIALS IN RESTRICTED SPACES

The art of sowing in limited spaces demands meticulous planning, foresight, and a deep understanding of the specific requirements of crops. As a farm owner, recognizing the critical aspects of sowing can set the foundation for a productive growing season.

Seed Quality and Selection

In the realm of agriculture, particularly when dealing with restricted spaces, the choice of starting materials plays an integral role in determining the outcome of the crop. Seed quality becomes paramount. The confined nature of limited spaces makes it crucial to optimize every factor, and seed quality stands at the foundation of these factors.

Optimized Utilization of Space: Premium quality seeds are likely to have higher germination rates. This ensures that the limited space is not wasted on seeds that never sprout.

Enhanced Disease Resistance: High-quality seeds often exhibit better resistance to diseases. In restricted spaces, diseases can spread rapidly due to the proximity of plants. By selecting disease-resistant seeds, one can reduce the risk of widespread plant ailments.

Yield Consistency: Seeds of good quality tend to produce plants that bear consistent yields. In spaces where every square inch matters, ensuring each plant is productive is of the essence.

Factors Determining Seed Quality

Seed quality isn't a singular attribute; it's an amalgamation of several factors that come together to ensure the seed's viability and the plant's future health.

Genetic Purity: This refers to the seed's inherent genetic makeup. A seed of high genetic purity will produce a plant that conforms to the expected type, with consistent characteristics.

Physical Quality: This encompasses the seed's appearance and health. Seeds should be free from damage, appropriately matured, and devoid of deformities.

Physiological Quality: A seed's vigor and viability fall under this category. Essentially, this measures the seed's potential for rapid and uniform germination and robust seedling growth.

Health: This criterion evaluates the seed's freedom from disease-causing pathogens, which might hinder germination or introduce diseases into the new growth environment.

Analytical Purity: Refers to the ratio of the desired seed to other seeds or impurities in a given sample. High analytical purity ensures that what you're sowing is indeed what you intended.

Selecting Seeds for Restricted Spaces

Determine Desired Outcomes: Before diving into seed selection, outline the goals. Are you aiming for a high yield, specific flavor profiles, ornamental value, or perhaps a combination of these? Your objectives will guide the selection process.

Opt for Dwarf or Compact Varieties: Many plants have dwarf or compact versions bred specifically for smaller spaces. These varieties tend to grow shorter and more bushy, making them ideal for confined areas without compromising on yield.

Research Disease Resistance: Especially for greenhouses or indoor gardens, select varieties that boast resistance to common diseases. This proactive approach can save a lot of time and resources in future plant care.

Consider Growth Duration: In restricted spaces, quick turnaround can be advantageous. Opting for seeds of plants that have shorter growth cycles allows for more crop rotations in a year, maximizing the yield from the limited space.

SEED PREPARATION TECHNIQUES

Seed preparation holds significant sway in agricultural success, especially in the unique context of limited spaces. In such scenarios, the importance of starting with a seed that's primed to yield the best possible growth cannot be overstated. Let us delve deeper into the intricate aspects of seed preparation techniques that can be harnessed to ensure an optimal start in confined farming environments.

Understanding Seed Preparation's Role

The role of seed preparation transcends just ensuring germination; it's a comprehensive approach to bolster the entire life cycle of a plant. When seeds are prepared correctly, they:

- Achieve quicker and more uniform germination.

- Stand a lower risk of succumbing to diseases at the nascent stages.

- Lead to plants that manifest better resilience and robustness, both crucial traits when working within restricted spaces.

Seed Cleaning: Beyond Basic Purification

Clean seeds are more than just aesthetically appealing; they promise accuracy in sowing, which is invaluable in limited spaces. When seeds are cleaned, they are rid of extraneous plant material such as chaff, ensuring that what goes into the ground (or growing medium) is pure, potent, and primed for growth.

Modern farm owners often employ seed cleaning machines for larger batches. These machines leverage screens and air currents to segregate seeds based on weight and size. Beyond large-scale operations, even smaller batches benefit from meticulous cleaning, be it through sieves or simple manual methods.

Breaking Boundaries with Seed Scarification

Certain seeds come with notably hard coats that can impede the absorption of water, delaying germination. Scarification is a technique tailored to tackle this, essentially breaking or softening the seed coat.

While there are mechanized methods to scarify seeds, traditional methods like using sandpaper or soaking seeds in hot water remain popular. In restricted spaces where every moment counts, scarified seeds offer the advantage of speed. They break ground faster, ensuring that limited spaces are continuously productive.

The Nuances of Seed Stratification

Nature, in its wisdom, has designed certain seeds to remain dormant until conditions are right. Stratification simulates these conditions, nudging seeds out of their dormancy. The essence of stratification, be it cold or warm, is to mirror the natural conditions a seed might experience in the wild over seasons.

Cold stratification, often achieved by refrigerating seeds mixed with a moist medium, is the more common technique. However, certain seeds benefit from a warm period before the cold treatment, necessitating warm stratification. When farming in limited spaces, stratification becomes indispensable. It orchestrates synchronized growth, leading to even canopy development which ensures equitable light distribution and resource consumption.

Delving into Seed Priming

Seed priming is akin to giving seeds a "head start". The seeds are soaked in solutions to initiate the metabolic processes associated with germination. However, the process is halted before the seed sprouts. This ensures that when such seeds are sown, they germinate rapidly and uniformly.

There are varied techniques within seed priming. Hydro-priming involves soaking seeds in pure water, while osmo-priming uses osmotic solutions, and matric priming leverages solid substrates. In the context of restricted spaces, primed seeds are invaluable. Uniform and rapid germination ensures that every inch of space is used efficiently, leading to consistent plant growth and yields.

The Protective Umbrella of Seed Disinfection

Diseases and pathogens are the bane of any farming operation, and more so in confined areas where they can spread rapidly. Seed disinfection serves as the first line of defense against these threats. By treating seeds to eliminate potential pathogens on their coat, we can curtail the introduction of diseases into the growing space.

Hot water treatments are commonly used, immersing seeds in water at specific temperatures. Chemical treatments, while effective, should be approached with caution, keeping in mind residue limits and potential ecological impacts.

The Art of Seed Pelleting and Coating

There's a finesse to seed pelleting and coating. Encasing seeds in a layer of inert material or providing them with nutrients not only makes them easier to handle but also primes them for better growth. Pelleted seeds, owing to their uniform shape, facilitate precision in sowing. Coated seeds, enriched with nutrients or growth promoters, offer plants a jump-start, a boon in restricted spaces where early growth dynamics can set the tone for the entire growth cycle.

In the vast tapestry of farming, seeds are the starting threads, and how these threads are treated and prepared can determine the design's intricacy and beauty. Seed preparation techniques, especially in restricted spaces, are not mere procedural steps but an amalgamation of art and science. Each technique, be it cleaning or priming, has a profound impact on the subsequent stages of plant growth. As modern farm owners, understanding and mastering these techniques becomes not just a choice, but a necessity, setting the stage for successful, bountiful harvests even in the most confined spaces.

SOIL AND MEDIA PREPARATION

In the realm of agriculture, soil is not merely a backdrop; it's an active player, a living entity that provides the fundamental framework for plant growth. But as we transition into modern farming practices, especially in restricted spaces, the canvas broadens. We now speak not just of soil but of growth media – diverse substances that can support plant life. In such settings, the preparation of soil and growth media evolves into an intricate dance, balancing the needs of the plants with the practicalities of the environment.

The Pillars of Optimal Soil Structure

The tactile quality of soil – its texture and structure – governs its behavior. A soil's texture, dictated by the proportions of sand, silt, and clay, impacts its water retention, aeration, and nutrient availability.

1. **Sandy Soil**: Characterized by larger particles, it ensures good aeration, but its rapid drainage can sometimes be a double-edged sword in restricted spaces, necessitating frequent watering.

2. **Silty Soil**: This soil, with its fine particles, offers a soft structure, holding moisture well. It can be prone to compaction, so careful management is crucial.

3. **Clayey Soil**: Renowned for its nutrient-rich nature, it holds water efficiently. However, its dense structure can hinder root penetration and reduce aeration.

In restricted spaces, achieving an optimal blend of these components is crucial. While natural topsoil can be a starting point, customizing the blend often becomes necessary. This may involve the addition of coarse sand to improve drainage or organic matter to enhance structure and nutrient content.

The Organic Infusion: The Role of Compost and Manure

Beyond the inorganic components, soil teems with life. Organic amendments, like compost and manure, serve multiple purposes. They introduce beneficial microorganisms, provide a steady supply of nutrients, and improve soil structure.

Compost, derived from decomposed plant material, offers a balanced nutrient profile. Its incorporation into the soil ensures sustained nutrient release, vital in restricted spaces where every square inch counts. Manure, on the other hand, offers a potent nutrient boost. However, it's essential to ensure that it's well-composted to prevent the risk of pathogens.

Growth Media: Beyond Traditional Soil

In modern, confined agricultural spaces, the traditional notion of soil is sometimes replaced or complemented by alternative growth media. The reasons are manifold: better control over nutrient content, superior aeration, faster growth, and sometimes, sheer necessity due to the absence of soil.

1. **Coir**: Derived from coconut husks, coir is a renewable medium, offering excellent water retention and aeration.

2. **Perlite**: This volcanic rock provides a lightweight, aerated medium. Its porous nature ensures good moisture retention, making it a favored choice in hydroponics.

3. **Vermiculite**: This silicate mineral expands upon heating, resulting in a lightweight, absorbent medium, beneficial for seed starting.

The choice of growth media often hinges on the specific requirements of the plants and the constraints of the restricted space.

Tackling Soil-Borne Diseases

Diseases are the unseen adversaries in any agricultural venture. In confined spaces, where plants grow in proximity, the risk is amplified. Soil sterilization emerges as a pivotal step in countering this.

Solarization, achieved by covering moist soil with clear plastic and exposing it to sunlight, allows heat to permeate and neutralize pathogens. Alternatively, biofumigation, employing certain plants like mustard, releases natural compounds into the soil, suppressing harmful organisms.

Balancing Soil pH and Nutrient Levels

Plants, much like humans, have preferences. Some thrive in acidic conditions, others in alkaline. Striking the right pH balance is paramount. Lime can raise the soil pH, making it more alkaline, while substances like sulfur or pine needles can be used to lower pH, increasing acidity.

Furthermore, a regular assessment of nutrient levels ensures that plants have access to the necessary macro and micronutrients. Depending on the findings, supplemental fertilizers, either synthetic or organic, can be incorporated.

Root Zone Management in Restricted Spaces

In confined agricultural spaces, root zone management assumes a critical role. It's not just about ensuring adequate space but also about orchestrating an environment where roots can breathe, access nutrients, and stay disease-free.

Good drainage is essential. Whether it's ensuring the right soil texture, installing drainage layers, or customizing pots with optimal hole sizes, the goal remains consistent: no waterlogging, no root rot.

Embracing Modern Innovations

Advances in agricultural science have ushered in novel soil additives and growth media. Biochar, a form of charcoal infused into the soil, can improve water retention and provide a habitat for beneficial microbes. Mycorrhizal fungi, when introduced, form symbiotic relationships with plant roots, enhancing nutrient uptake.

SOWING TECHNIQUES FOR LIMITED SPACES

The precision with which seeds are sown in a farm dictates the quality of the subsequent harvest. The intricacies become even more pronounced when working within restricted spaces. Every square inch is invaluable, and the techniques employed must maximize yield while ensuring the health and vigor of each plant.

Understanding the Significance of Spacing

Spacing is more than just an aesthetic preference; it's a strategic decision with repercussions on plant health and yield. Crowded plants compete for resources, with intertwined roots and overshadowed leaves. Proper spacing optimizes airflow, minimizes disease transmission, and ensures that each plant receives its fair share of sunlight and nutrients.

In restricted areas, it's tempting to squeeze in as many seeds as possible, but this can be counterproductive. It's pivotal to acquaint oneself with the spatial needs of each crop and sow seeds in a manner that ensures room for growth without wastage of space.

Direct Sowing versus Transplanting

There's an ongoing debate regarding the merits of direct sowing versus transplanting, and both methods have their place in restricted farming.

Direct sowing involves placing seeds directly where they'll grow to maturity. It reduces transplant shock and is often more straightforward. However, it might not always be feasible in very confined spaces, especially for crops that need a longer growing season.

Transplanting, or starting seeds in trays and transferring them to their final location once they've established, provides more control over the initial growth environment. It ensures that only the healthiest seedlings are selected for final planting, maximizing the chances of a successful harvest. For limited spaces, transplanting can be a boon, allowing farm owners to stagger plantings and ensure a continuous harvest.

Delving into the Depth of Sowing

How deep a seed is sown can influence its germination rate. Too shallow, and the seed risks drying out or becoming fodder for birds. Too deep, and the young seedling might exhaust its energy reserves before reaching sunlight.

The general rule of thumb is to sow a seed at a depth approximately twice its diameter. However, some seeds, especially those of light-sensitive plants, prefer surface sowing. These nuances are vital to recognize, especially in restricted spaces where every seed counts.

Embracing Succession Sowing

One of the tricks to maximize yield in limited spaces is succession sowing. It refers to the practice of planting seeds at staggered intervals, ensuring a steady stream of produce rather than a single, overwhelming harvest.

For instance, instead of sowing all lettuce seeds at once, they can be sown every two weeks. This way, as one batch is harvested, another is ready to take its place, ensuring a constant supply. The practice not only maximizes space utilization but also ensures fresh produce availability over an extended period.

Vertical Sowing: Rising Above the Ground

Not all sowing needs to be horizontal. Vertical sowing techniques, which involve growing plants upwards using supports, trellises, or hanging containers, can be a game-changer in confined spaces. Crops like beans, tomatoes, and certain squash varieties naturally lend themselves to vertical growth.

Such an approach not only saves ground space but also improves air circulation, reducing the risk of fungal diseases. Additionally, vertical growth can make pest management more straightforward, as many pests find it challenging to navigate heights.

Incorporating Companion Planting

Companion planting, the practice of sowing complementary plants together, can be particularly advantageous in limited spaces. Certain plant combinations benefit each other by improving soil health, deterring pests, or enhancing growth.

For instance, marigolds, when sown alongside tomatoes, can deter nematodes. Beans, being nitrogen-fixing plants, can enrich the soil for neighboring crops that demand high nitrogen.

By understanding these symbiotic relationships, farm owners can design a sowing plan that not only maximizes space but also enhances overall crop health and yield.

Optimizing for Light and Airflow

When planning sowing in a restricted area, it's essential to account for the sunlight and airflow needs of each crop. Taller plants can overshadow shorter ones if not strategically placed. Similarly, crops that are prone to fungal diseases need more airflow and should be positioned accordingly.

Given the constraints, sometimes it becomes necessary to employ techniques like pruning or training plants to grow in a specific direction to ensure that every plant gets its share of resources.

The Role of Containers in Sowing

Containers play an indispensable role in restricted space farming. They offer the flexibility to move plants around, optimizing sunlight exposure. The choice of container, its size, depth, and material can influence plant growth. A container too small can constrict root growth, while one too large might lead to waterlogging.

The Nuances of Seed Varieties

Lastly, it's essential to note that not all seed varieties are created equal. Some are explicitly bred for confined spaces, offering dwarf varieties or those with compact growth habits. Such seeds can be a boon for restricted space farming, allowing farm owners to get the most out of every square inch.

In conclusion, sowing in restricted spaces is both an art and a science. It demands a deep understanding of plant needs, spatial dynamics, and the ability to innovate. With the right techniques, even the most confined spaces can be transformed into lush, productive gardens, offering bountiful harvests and the satisfaction of optimized growth.

MONITORING AND MANAGEMENT POST-SOWING

The act of sowing seeds, while pivotal, is only the beginning of the journey in restricted space agriculture. What follows is a dynamic phase of monitoring and management to ensure that these seeds not only germinate but also thrive, leading to a productive yield. Delving into this next phase, we unearth the essentials of post-sowing care, especially tailored for limited spaces.

The First Watch: Germination Monitoring

As the seeds settle into their new environment, the immediate focus turns to germination. The time it takes for a seed to sprout can vary significantly depending on its type, the environmental conditions, and the quality of the seed. This period demands patience but also a vigilant eye.

- Moisture Level: Consistent moisture is critical for seed germination. Too wet and the seed can rot; too dry and it may not germinate at all. It's essential to strike a balance. In confined spaces, there might be less natural evaporation, so be mindful of over-watering. A simple touch-test can often indicate if the soil's surface needs a light misting or if it's adequately moist.

☐ Temperature: While some seeds can germinate over a wide temperature range, others have specific needs. It's prudent to be aware of these requirements, and if necessary, employ heated mats or utilize cooler areas in the space to provide optimal conditions.

Tending to the Tenderlings: Seedling Care

Once the seedlings break through the soil, they enter a vulnerable phase. These young plants, while filled with potential, can easily succumb to a range of issues if not monitored and managed appropriately.

☐ Light Requirements: Seedlings require ample light to grow strong and healthy. In limited spaces, ensuring consistent light might mean the introduction of artificial grow lights. These lights can be adjusted in intensity and duration to mimic the ideal daylight conditions.

☐ Thinning Out: It's not uncommon to sow more seeds than required, anticipating some may not germinate. However, once seedlings appear, it might become evident that there's overcrowding. Thinning out, or selectively removing weaker seedlings, ensures that the remaining ones have adequate space to grow.

Nutrition and Growth: Fertilization Strategy

A robust plant is a well-fed one. As the seedlings grow, their nutritional demands increase. In confined farming spaces, the soil or growth medium's nutrient content might deplete faster due to the higher plant density.

☐ Regular Monitoring: Keep a close eye on plant color and vigor as indicators of nutritional health. Yellowing leaves, stunted growth, or poor root development might indicate a deficiency.

☐ Tailored Nutrition: Different plants have varying nutrient requirements. A tomato plant's nutritional needs differ from lettuce. Understanding these specific needs and applying tailored fertilizers can make all the difference in yield quality and quantity.

Disease and Pest Vigilance

The restricted environment of confined spaces can sometimes become a haven for pests and diseases. The close proximity of plants to each other facilitates the rapid spread of issues.

☐ Regular Inspections: It's wise to set aside dedicated time to inspect plants for signs of pests or diseases. Look under leaves, around stems, and even in the soil. Early detection is the key to effective management.

☐ Integrated Pest Management (IPM): Instead of relying solely on chemicals, consider an IPM approach. This method combines cultural, biological, and chemical strategies to manage pests in a more sustainable and effective manner.

Managing Microclimates

In restricted spaces, small changes in the environment can create microclimates. These are localized atmospheric zones where the temperature, humidity, or light might differ from the surrounding areas.

- Proper Ventilation: Ensure that the space has adequate ventilation. This not only regulates temperature and moisture but also prevents the buildup of pathogens.

- Use of Reflective Materials: In areas where light is scarce, reflective materials can be utilized to bounce back sunlight or artificial light, ensuring even distribution.

Training and Pruning for Growth

As plants grow, they might require guidance in their growth direction, especially in confined spaces.

- Support Systems: Employ trellises, stakes, or cages to support plants that have a vining or tall growth habit. This not only optimizes space but also ensures plants grow healthily.

- Pruning: Strategic pruning can redirect a plant's energy to desired areas. For fruiting plants, this can lead to better yields. For ornamental plants, it can shape them aesthetically.

In restricted spaces, the margin for error narrows, making the post-sowing phase even more critical. Each step, from germination monitoring to mature plant care, must be executed with precision and knowledge. It's a dance of science and intuition, understanding plant signals, and responding in kind. And when done right, even the most confined spaces can yield results that rival expansive farms, bearing testimony to the prowess of meticulous monitoring and management.

SEED STORAGE FOR FUTURE SOWING

Storing seeds for future sowing is more than just placing them in a container and setting them aside. Proper seed storage is a nuanced process, a combination of art and science, and is essential for ensuring seed viability and maintaining genetic diversity. For a modern farm owner, particularly one operating within restricted spaces, mastering the techniques of seed storage becomes paramount to ensure a consistent and healthy crop rotation year-round.

Understanding Seed Viability

Before diving into the specifics of storage, it's crucial to grasp the concept of seed viability. Seeds are living entities, and like all living things, they have a lifespan. The viability of a seed refers to its ability to germinate and produce a vigorous plant. The length of time a seed remains viable depends on the seed type and the conditions in which it's stored.

The Four Pillars of Seed Storage

There are four primary factors to consider when storing seeds: temperature, humidity, light, and air. Each plays a vital role in extending seed viability.

1. **Temperature:** Most seeds have a preferred storage temperature that maximizes their lifespan. Generally, cooler temperatures are better, with many seeds storing well at temperatures just above freezing. However, it's essential to avoid extreme temperature fluctuations, as this can harm the seed's cellular structure.

2. **Humidity:** Moisture is a seed's enemy during storage. Excessive humidity can trigger premature germination or cause seeds to rot. Using desiccants or moisture-absorbing packets in storage containers can help maintain a low humidity environment.

3. **Light:** Exposure to light can reduce seed viability, especially for extended periods. As such, seeds should be stored in a dark place or in opaque containers.

4. **Air:** While seeds need oxygen to germinate, during storage, it's beneficial to reduce their exposure to air. Vacuum-sealing seeds or storing them in airtight containers can be effective in prolonging their viability.

Choosing the Right Storage Containers

The choice of storage container can significantly influence the condition of stored seeds.

☐ **Glass Jars:** These are a popular choice due to their airtight nature when sealed. They also protect seeds from pests. However, they should be stored in a dark place to prevent light exposure.

☐ **Mylar Bags:** These are effective in blocking out light and can be sealed tightly. When combined with desiccants, they provide an excellent storage environment.

☐ **Envelopes and Paper Bags:** While not as protective as other options, they can be useful for short-term storage or if seeds are stored in a larger, protective container. Their porous nature allows any residual moisture to escape, reducing the risk of mold.

Labeling and Documentation

It's not enough to simply store seeds; it's also imperative to document what's been stored. Over time, seeds can be easily mixed up or forgotten, leading to confusion during planting season.

☐ Each container should be clearly labeled with the seed type, variety, and date of storage. If known, noting the seed's origin and any other pertinent information can also be beneficial.

- Maintain a ledger or digital database of all stored seeds. This not only aids in organization but also helps in tracking seed viability over time.

Seed Storage Duration and Rotation

Different seeds have varying shelf lives. While some seeds, like parsnips, may only remain viable for a year or two, others, such as tomatoes or lettuce, can last several years if stored correctly.

- Regularly review stored seeds and prioritize using older seeds first.

- Conduct germination tests periodically on older seeds to ensure they're still viable. This involves placing a number of seeds between damp paper towels to see if they sprout.

Special Considerations for Restricted Spaces

When operating within limited spaces, optimizing storage becomes even more critical. Here are some tailored strategies:

- **Vertical Storage:** Utilize vertical space efficiently by employing shelving units or hanging storage solutions.

- **Climate Control:** In spaces where temperature and humidity can fluctuate, consider investing in a climate-controlled storage unit or cabinet.

- **Maximizing Space:** Store seeds in uniform containers, which can be stacked or arranged efficiently, to maximize storage space.

For the forward-thinking farm owner, seed storage is a long-term investment. It's a commitment to future harvests, to genetic diversity, and to the continuity of agricultural practices. In restricted spaces, the challenge intensifies, but with meticulous attention to detail, knowledge of seeds, and a structured approach, it's more than feasible to store seeds effectively, ensuring a bountiful yield season after season.

ENGAGING WITH THE COMMUNITY

Farming, while often imagined as an isolated endeavor, is deeply interwoven with the community it serves. Even in the context of restricted space farming, the connection between the farm and the local community remains robust and mutually beneficial. This relationship is essential not just from an economic standpoint but also for fostering a sense of belonging, sharing knowledge, and promoting sustainable practices. Engaging with the community can yield dividends for the modern farm owner that extend far beyond immediate profit margins.

Community Engagement as a Two-Way Street

Engagement is not a one-sided affair where the farm owner dictates terms or merely advertises produce. It's about active listening, understanding the community's needs, and positioning the farm as a responsive entity, ready to adapt and provide.

Knowledge Sharing Sessions

One of the most direct ways to engage with the community is through knowledge sharing. Organizing regular sessions where community members can learn about farming practices, particularly those unique to restricted space farming, can be immensely beneficial.

These sessions not only allow the community to understand the challenges and intricacies of modern farming but also highlight the quality and effort put into the produce they consume. It creates a sense of trust, and in many cases, a willing preference for locally produced goods over imported ones.

Furthermore, these sessions can become platforms for exchange. Local residents may possess generational knowledge, indigenous farming techniques, or even feedback that can aid the farm's operation.

Collaborative Farming Initiatives

Another effective engagement strategy is to initiate collaborative farming projects. These could range from community gardening plots within the farm's vicinity to collaborative planting days where community members are invited to participate in sowing sessions. Such initiatives provide hands-on experience and foster a sense of collective ownership and pride in the produce.

This approach not only deepens the bond between the farm and the community but also serves as an educational tool, especially for younger generations. It can instill values of hard work, patience, and appreciation for the agricultural process.

Pop-Up Markets and Direct Selling

Selling directly to the community can be a game-changer. Organizing pop-up markets or farm-to-table events allows the community to interact directly with the source of their food. This transparency builds trust and often results in increased loyalty from consumers.

Direct selling events can also be occasions for feedback. Understanding the community's preferences, dietary needs, or even logistical feedback about market timings and produce varieties can shape the farm's future strategies.

Engagement Through Technology

In today's digital age, community engagement isn't limited to physical interactions. Establishing a robust online presence through social media platforms, interactive websites, or community forums can amplify the farm's reach and engagement.

By posting regular updates, sharing behind-the-scenes glimpses, or even conducting virtual farm tours, the modern farm owner can engage with a broader audience. Online platforms also provide avenues for instant feedback, queries, and suggestions, making the engagement process dynamic and real-time.

Partnerships with Local Establishments

Another facet of community engagement is forming partnerships with local businesses or establishments. Collaborating with local restaurants, cafes, or grocery stores can establish a steady demand for the farm's produce. But beyond mere business transactions, these partnerships can amplify the ethos of restricted space farming.

For instance, a local cafe can host monthly farm-themed events or dishes that highlight the farm's produce, complete with information about its sourcing and benefits. Such collaborations create a web of interdependence, strengthening the entire community's economic and social fabric.

Educational Programs for Schools

Engaging with schools and educational institutions offers another layer of community interaction. Offering field trips, workshops, or even curriculum-based programs can instill agricultural appreciation in students. Given the unique nature of restricted space farming, students gain insights into innovative farming practices, resource optimization, and sustainable agriculture.

Addressing Community Concerns

It's crucial to note that community engagement isn't always positive. There might be concerns or apprehensions about certain farming practices, water usage, or even the aesthetic aspect of having a farm in a restricted space. Addressing these concerns proactively, ensuring open lines of communication, and making necessary adjustments showcases the farm's commitment to the community's well-being.

In essence, a modern farm, irrespective of its size or location, doesn't operate in a vacuum. It's a vital component of the community ecosystem. By actively engaging with the community, the farm owner does more than just sell produce. They build relationships, foster trust, and most importantly, they weave the farm's narrative into the community's story. The intertwined futures of both the farm and the community highlight the importance of consistent and meaningful engagement.

UNDERSTANDING SEASON EXTENSION

Season extension is an indispensable strategy for modern farm owners who aim to maximize yield, especially in limited spaces. By manipulating the environment, one can create conditions that allow crops to grow outside their regular growing season.

THE SIGNIFICANCE OF MICROCLIMATES

Identifying Microclimates: Every garden or farm has microclimates—small areas where conditions vary from the overall climate due to factors such as sunlight, wind, or proximity to buildings. Recognizing these areas can help in placing crops that might benefit from these specific conditions.

Maximizing Microclimates: For example, a south-facing wall in the Northern Hemisphere can provide additional warmth and protection from winds. Placing cold-sensitive plants in such a location can extend their growth period.

GREENHOUSES AND HOOPHOUSES

The Basics: Greenhouses and hoophouses are structures, either temporary or permanent, designed to trap heat. They protect plants from extreme cold, wind, and in some cases, pests.

Types and Materials: Materials for these structures range from glass, polycarbonate panels to UV-resistant plastic. The choice depends on budget, space, and the degree of temperature control needed.

Ventilation: While retaining heat is the primary goal, ventilation is essential to prevent overheating during sunny days. Properly placed vents, manual or automatic, maintain temperature and humidity at desired levels.

Heating Options: For extremely cold regions, additional heating might be required. Heaters, whether electric or gas-powered, can be installed, but they should be used judiciously to maintain sustainability.

COLD FRAMES AND CLOCHES

Cold Frames: A cold frame is a bottomless box with a transparent top. It's positioned directly on the ground, capturing warmth from the sun, and acting as a miniature greenhouse.

Cloches: Traditionally bell-shaped, cloches are transparent or semi-transparent covers placed over individual plants. They can be made of plastic, glass, or fabric.

Management: Both cold frames and cloches should be monitored to ensure plants don't overheat. On sunny days, it might be necessary to prop them open for ventilation.

ROW COVERS AND SHADE CLOTHES

Row Covers: Made of lightweight polyester or polypropylene, row covers can protect plants from frost, wind, and pests. They allow light and rain to penetrate while elevating daytime temperatures.

Shade Clothes: During hot seasons, shade clothes protect plants from intense sunlight. Depending on the crop, shade cloths with varying degrees of light blockage can be chosen.

MULCHING FOR TEMPERATURE REGULATION

Organic Mulches: Materials like straw, leaves, or wood chips can be spread around plants. They conserve moisture, suppress weeds, and regulate soil temperature.

Plastic Mulches: These are plastic sheets laid on planting beds. While black plastic mulch retains heat, reflective ones can deter pests. However, plastic mulches must be used responsibly considering environmental concerns.

SOIL WARMING TECHNIQUES

Raised Beds: Raised garden beds warm up faster than ground-level soils in spring. This characteristic can accelerate planting schedules.

Thermal Mass: Water containers, rocks, or bricks placed strategically can absorb heat during the day and release it at night, moderating temperature fluctuations.

Soil Heating Cables: Electric cables, when buried in the soil, can raise its temperature, ensuring optimal root growth in cold months.

UTILIZING SUCCESSION PLANTING

Staggering plantings at intervals can ensure a continuous harvest throughout the season. As one crop concludes its growth cycle, another batch is ready to take its place, ensuring maximized use of available space.

SELECTION OF VARIETIES

Choosing early-maturing or cold-tolerant varieties can further extend the season. These varieties are specifically bred to withstand sub-optimal conditions and can offer a harvest when standard varieties might falter.

WATER MANAGEMENT

Drip Irrigation: In limited spaces, drip irrigation ensures water is delivered directly to plant roots, reducing evaporation and wastage.

Rainwater Harvesting: Collecting rainwater in barrels or tanks can provide an additional water source during dry spells, ensuring plants remain hydrated.

Frost Protection: Watering plants in the evening can help protect them from frost. As water releases heat more slowly than dry soil, it can keep plants slightly warmer during frosty nights.

WINDBREAKS AND BARRIERS

Wind can significantly affect temperature. Installing temporary or permanent windbreaks, such as netting, fences, or even strategically placed plants, can shield sensitive crops from cold winds.

DATA MONITORING AND ANALYSIS

Digital Tools: Modern farm owners are increasingly leveraging technology. Sensors can monitor temperature, humidity, and soil moisture, sending real-time data to smartphones or computers.

Record Keeping: Maintaining detailed records of planting dates, harvest times, and weather conditions can help in refining strategies for subsequent years.

ADVANCED TECHNOLOGIES IN SEASON EXTENSION

Automated Systems: From greenhouses with automated ventilation and shading systems to soil moisture sensors that trigger irrigation, automation is revolutionizing season extension techniques.

Climate Prediction Tools: By analyzing weather data, some tools can provide forecasts tailored for agriculture, aiding farmers in making informed decisions.

ECONOMIC CONSIDERATIONS

While extending the season can enhance yields, it's essential to evaluate the economic feasibility. Costs incurred in infrastructure, heating, or additional resources should be weighed against the potential increase in revenue from extended harvests.

Extending the season in limited spaces is both an art and science. By melding traditional methods with modern innovations, today's farm owner can ensure a prolonged, productive growing season. This extended season not only amplifies potential profits but also contributes to food security by providing fresh produce beyond the standard growing months. As urbanization continues and available farming space becomes premium, these strategies will be invaluable in shaping the future of sustainable agriculture.

FRUIT TREES AND VINES

STRATEGIC SELECTION OF FRUIT VARIETIES

Dwarf and Semi-Dwarf Varieties: Modern farm owners recognize the value of dwarf and semi-dwarf fruit tree varieties. These trees are genetically designed to attain only a fraction of their full-sized counterparts' height, making them ideal for confined spaces. For instance, dwarf apple trees can yield substantial amounts of fruit without demanding expansive orchard spaces.

Columnar Fruit Trees: Columnar or 'fastigiate' trees have a naturally upright growth habit. An excellent example is the columnar apple. These trees require minimal horizontal space, focusing growth vertically and are especially suited to narrow areas or even large containers.

Grafted Multi-Fruit Trees: Grafting allows multiple fruit varieties on a single tree. This means a tree could potentially yield plums, apricots, and peaches all at once. Such trees are a boon for limited space, offering diverse harvests without the spatial demands of multiple trees.

OPTIMIZING SPACE WITH ESPALIER TECHNIQUES

Understanding Espalier: Espalier is the art and science of training trees to grow against a flat surface, typically in patterned forms. The tree is pruned and trained to grow in one plane, offering both aesthetic appeal and space efficiency.

Espalier Forms: There are various forms, including the candelabra, fan, and horizontal cordon. The choice depends on the tree species and the aesthetic or space requirement.

Maintenance: Espaliered trees need regular pruning to maintain their form. It's essential to understand the growth habits of the chosen fruit tree to ensure optimal fruit production alongside the desired shape.

VINES: VERTICAL GROWTH MAXIMIZES OUTPUT

Types of Fruit Vines: From grapes, kiwifruits to passion fruits, vines naturally seek vertical growth. They can be trained to grow upwards on trellises, fences, or walls, making the best use of available vertical space.

Trellising Systems: The type of trellising system chosen can affect fruit production and ease of harvest. Systems such as the single wire, double wire, or Geneva Double Curtain are designed to support the weight of the vine and fruit, ensuring sunlight and air circulation for all parts of the vine.

Pruning for Productivity: Regular pruning is crucial for vines. This not only maintains the vine's form but also directs energy towards fruit production. Proper pruning ensures good fruit size, faster ripening, and easier harvest.

CONTAINER-GROWN FRUIT TREES AND VINES

Choosing the Right Container: The container's size and material can influence root health. It's imperative to ensure adequate drainage and choose a size that allows roots ample space to grow.

Soil and Nutrition: Container-grown plants don't have the luxury of sourcing nutrients beyond their confined space. Use a high-quality potting mix, enriched with compost. Regularly monitor nutrient levels, replenishing as needed.

Watering Regimen: Containers can dry out faster than ground soil. Implementing a consistent watering regimen, possibly aided by drip irrigation or self-watering systems, ensures the plants don't suffer water stress.

MICROCLIMATES: HARNESSING FOR FRUIT PRODUCTION

Understanding Site-specific Conditions: Even within limited spaces, there can be variations in temperature, wind exposure, and sunlight. These are microclimates. Recognizing these can guide where to place fruit trees and vines for optimal growth.

Utilizing Structures: Walls, fences, and even paved surfaces can reflect heat, creating warmer zones. These spots can be advantageous for heat-loving fruits, extending their growing season.

MAINTENANCE AND PEST CONTROL

Regular Pruning: Pruning not only shapes the tree but also encourages better air circulation and light penetration. This reduces the risk of fungal diseases and ensures better fruit quality.

Integrated Pest Management (IPM): Adopt IPM strategies to keep pests at bay. This might involve introducing beneficial insects, using pheromone traps, or applying organic pesticides judiciously.

Monitoring and Early Intervention: Regularly inspect trees and vines for signs of diseases or pests. Early detection and intervention can prevent minor issues from escalating into major problems.

POLLINATION CONSIDERATIONS

Self-pollinating vs. Cross-pollinating: Some fruit trees and vines are self-pollinating, requiring no external agent for fruit set. Others might require cross-pollination. In limited spaces, it's crucial to understand these requirements.

Encouraging Pollinators: Promote bee and insect activity by planting flowers and maintaining a pesticide-free environment. Alternatively, in extremely confined spaces, consider hand pollination.

TRAINING AND SUPPORTING VINES

Guiding Growth: Vines can be trained to grow in specific patterns or directions. Use soft ties to guide young shoots, ensuring they grow in the desired direction.

Support Structures: Ensure trellises, stakes, or netting are sturdy enough to bear the weight of mature vines laden with fruit. Periodically inspect and repair these structures to prevent collapses.

HARVESTING AND POST-HARVEST CARE

Recognizing Ripeness: Different fruits have distinct ripeness indicators. From a change in color, softness, or ease of detachment, knowing when to harvest ensures the best flavor and texture.

Storage and Preservation: Limited space farming often results in staggered harvests. Understand the storage requirements of each fruit. Some might need refrigeration, while others might benefit from being kept at room temperature.

ADVANCED TECHNOLOGIES IN FRUIT PRODUCTION

Drip Irrigation Systems: Automated drip irrigation can deliver water right to the root zone, ensuring optimal moisture levels.

Soil Moisture Sensors: These sensors can indicate when the soil becomes too dry, signaling the need for watering. It's a crucial tool for container-grown fruit trees where moisture levels can fluctuate rapidly.

ECONOMIC CONSIDERATIONS FOR LIMITED SPACE FRUIT PRODUCTION

While the idea of producing fruits in confined spaces is enticing, it's essential to weigh the costs. Infrastructure, soil, containers, and potential yield should be factored into decisions to ensure that the endeavor remains both sustainable and profitable.

Growing fruit trees and vines in limited spaces requires a blend of traditional knowledge and innovative strategies. As urban spaces become more congested and the value of every square foot escalates, these techniques will be indispensable for modern farm owners and enthusiasts. With thoughtful planning, even the smallest spaces can become bountiful orchards, testifying to the marvels of modern horticulture.

MAXIMIZING YIELD IN SMALL SPACES

UNDERSTANDING PLANT DENSITY AND SPACING

Principles of Plant Density: In constrained spaces, plant density becomes a crucial factor. The number of plants per unit area can impact light availability, air circulation, and nutrient uptake.

Root Development and Soil Volume: Each plant species has a characteristic root system. Understand the space requirements for root development to avoid overcrowding and ensure optimal nutrient absorption.

Square Foot Gardening: Developed by Mel Bartholomew, this method divides garden beds into square-foot sections to efficiently use space and reduce walkways. The number of plants per square foot depends on the specific crop's requirements.

VERTICAL FARMING TECHNIQUES

Benefits of Vertical Growth: Vertical farming is not just for urban skyscrapers. Even in small gardens, growing upwards can significantly increase yield per square foot.

Use of Trellises and Netting: Crops like beans, peas, cucumbers, and tomatoes can be trained to grow upwards using trellises, stakes, and netting. This not only saves horizontal space but also improves air circulation, reducing fungal diseases.

Tiered Planting Systems: Multi-level planting platforms can host various plants, ensuring each level receives adequate sunlight. These systems are particularly suitable for shallow-rooted crops.

COMPANION PLANTING FOR ENHANCED PRODUCTIVITY

Symbiotic Relationships: Certain plant combinations can benefit one another. For example, tall corn can provide shade for heat-sensitive lettuce, while the lettuce covers the soil, suppressing weeds.

Pest Deterrence: Some plants release chemicals that deter pests. Interplanting these with susceptible crops can reduce pest problems without resorting to chemical interventions.

Nutrient Complementation: Legumes, like beans and peas, fix atmospheric nitrogen. Growing them alongside nitrogen-loving plants like corn can enhance soil fertility and yield.

SOIL HEALTH AND FERTILITY MANAGEMENT

Importance of Soil Structure: Loose, well-aerated soil promotes healthy root growth, ensuring optimal water and nutrient uptake. Regularly incorporate organic matter to improve soil structure.

Continuous Nutrient Supply: In high-density planting systems, nutrient competition is intense. Implement a balanced fertilization schedule, possibly using slow-release fertilizers or frequent, dilute applications of liquid fertilizers.

Beneficial Microorganisms: Inoculating the soil with beneficial fungi and bacteria can enhance nutrient availability and improve plant resilience against diseases.

EFFICIENT WATER MANAGEMENT

Drip Irrigation Systems: Delivering water directly to the root zone minimizes evaporation losses and ensures plants get the moisture they need, especially vital in dense plantings.

Mulching: Mulching with organic matter like straw or wood chips conserves soil moisture, suppresses weeds, and regulates soil temperature, fostering healthy plant growth.

Moisture Monitoring: Use moisture meters or simple manual checks to gauge soil wetness, ensuring plants receive water when needed, avoiding both waterlogging and drought stress.

PRUNING AND TRAINING FOR OPTIMAL LIGHT EXPOSURE

Benefits of Pruning: Removing select branches or leaves can improve light penetration and air movement, critical in densely planted areas. Pruning can also direct a plant's energy towards fruit or flower production.

Training Plants: Beyond vertical training, shaping plants to maximize sunlight capture can enhance photosynthesis and yield. For example, tomato plants can be trained as single-stemmed vines, allowing more plants per unit area.

SUCCESSION PLANTING AND CROP ROTATION

Continuous Harvests: By planting in intervals, one can ensure a continuous supply of produce. Once one crop is harvested, the next set of plants is ready to take its place.

Soil Health through Rotation: Different crops have varied nutrient requirements and pest profiles. Rotating them can prevent soil nutrient depletion and disrupt pest and disease cycles.

SEED SELECTION AND HYBRID VARIETIES

Fast-maturing Varieties: Opt for varieties that mature quickly, allowing for multiple plantings in a single growing season.

High-yield Hybrids: Modern agricultural research has led to the development of hybrid varieties designed for higher yields, disease resistance, and space efficiency.

Disease-resistant Strains: In dense plantings, the risk of disease transmission is high. Using disease-resistant plant varieties can mitigate this risk.

ADVANCED TECHNOLOGIES IN HIGH-DENSITY FARMING

Automated Planting Systems: Precision planters can ensure optimal spacing, reducing seed wastage and ensuring each plant has the space it needs.

Sensor-guided Watering: Incorporate sensors that detect soil moisture levels, directing irrigation systems to water only when necessary, optimizing water usage.

LED Grow Lights: In exceptionally space-restricted or indoor environments, LED grow lights can supplement or replace sunlight, ensuring plants receive the light spectrum they need for growth.

ENHANCING POLLINATION IN DENSE SETUPS

Encouraging Natural Pollinators: Incorporate flowering plants to attract bees, butterflies, and other pollinators, ensuring good fruit set.

Hand Pollination: In certain situations, especially indoors or in high-pollution areas, manual pollination using brushes or cotton swabs might be necessary.

INTEGRATED PEST MANAGEMENT (IPM) IN HIGH-DENSITY AREAS

Biological Control: Introduce beneficial insects like ladybugs and lacewings to control pest populations naturally.

Barrier Systems: Use floating row covers or netting to protect plants from pests, eliminating the need for chemical interventions.

Regular Monitoring: Inspect plants regularly for signs of pests or diseases. Early detection is key to managing potential outbreaks in dense plantings.

HARVESTING TECHNIQUES IN TIGHT QUARTERS

Timely Harvesting: Prompt harvesting at the right maturity stage ensures optimal flavor and nutrient content, and makes way for subsequent crops.

Gentle Handling: Densely grown crops might intertwine. Harvest with care to avoid damaging neighboring plants.

Maximizing yield in limited spaces is a harmonious blend of traditional farming knowledge, innovative techniques, and modern technology. Every inch of soil and every drop of water becomes precious. With attention to detail and a proactive approach, even the smallest plot can be transformed into a productive oasis, reflecting the possibilities of efficient and sustainable agriculture.

THE FUNDAMENTALS OF INTERCROPPING

Defining Intercropping: Intercropping is the agricultural practice of cultivating two or more crops in close proximity. The primary objective is to maximize the use of resources such as light, nutrients, and water by using the unique growth patterns and requirements of combined crops.

History and Origins: Historically, farmers have practiced intercropping to diversify their harvest, reduce risk, and improve yield. Ancient civilizations, such as those in Mesoamerica, combined maize, beans, and squash – known as the "Three Sisters" – for mutual benefits.

Types of Intercropping: Different patterns and combinations define various forms of intercropping:

- *Row Intercropping:* Crops are grown in alternating rows.

- *Mixed Intercropping:* Different crops are sown without a specific pattern.

- *Relay Intercropping:* A second crop is sown after the first has established, but before it is harvested.

ECOLOGICAL AND ENVIRONMENTAL BENEFITS

Enhanced Biodiversity: Intercropping can increase diversity within a plot, which can attract beneficial insects and reduce the prevalence of pests.

Soil Health and Conservation: Different crops have varied root systems and nutrient requirements. This can result in more efficient nutrient uptake and reduced soil erosion.

Pest and Disease Control: With a variety of crops, pests specific to one crop might be deterred by the presence of another. Additionally, the spread of disease can be minimized as pathogens often target specific plants.

RESOURCE OPTIMIZATION IN INTERCROPPING

Light Utilization: Taller crops can provide shade to shorter, shade-loving crops, ensuring optimal use of sunlight.

Soil Nutrient Management: Legumes can fix atmospheric nitrogen, benefiting adjacent nitrogen-loving plants. Deep-rooted crops can bring up nutrients from the soil depths, benefiting shallow-rooted companions.

Efficient Water Use: Plants with diverse water requirements can be paired, ensuring that water is utilized at different soil depths, reducing competition.

KEY CONSIDERATIONS FOR INTERCROPPING DESIGN

Growth Rate and Maturity: Plants with similar growth rates and maturity periods are often paired to ensure one doesn't overshadow the other.

Rooting Depth: Crops with different rooting depths are ideal, allowing them to access nutrients and water from different soil strata without competition.

Spatial Needs: Plants that spread, like melons, can be grown with upright plants, such as maize, to maximize space utilization.

MANAGEMENT PRACTICES IN INTERCROPPING

Sowing and Planting: Correct timing is vital. Some crops are planted simultaneously, while others might be staggered to ensure they don't compete during crucial growth stages.

Fertilization: Understanding the nutrient needs of each crop ensures balanced fertilization. Soil tests can be invaluable in guiding fertilizer application.

Irrigation: Water requirements for each crop should be considered. Drip irrigation systems can be tailored to deliver varying water quantities to different plants.

CHALLENGES IN INTERCROPPING

Competition: If not correctly managed, crops can compete for resources, reducing overall yield.

Harvesting Complications: Different maturity times can make harvesting more labor-intensive. Moreover, mechanized harvesting can be challenging in mixed crops.

Pest and Disease Transmission: While intercropping can deter pests, it's also possible for one crop to introduce pests or diseases that affect its partner.

MODERN INNOVATIONS AND RESEARCH IN INTERCROPPING

Precision Agriculture: With advancements in technology, farmers can use drones and sensors to monitor the health of intercropped fields, ensuring timely interventions.

Genetic Improvements: Research is ongoing to develop crop varieties specifically designed for intercropping systems, focusing on compatibility and resource-sharing.

Advanced Irrigation Systems: Modern irrigation systems can be programmed to provide different amounts of water to different crops, optimizing water use in intercropped fields.

ECONOMIC IMPLICATIONS OF INTERCROPPING

Risk Mitigation: If one crop fails due to environmental reasons or market fluctuations, the other can provide financial security.

Enhanced Productivity: When practiced correctly, intercropping can increase yield per unit area, leading to higher profitability.

Labor and Input Costs: Intercropping might require more intensive management, potentially increasing labor costs. However, these costs can be offset by the reduced need for chemical inputs and the benefits of diversified produce.

CASE STUDIES: SUCCESSFUL INTERCROPPING MODELS WORLDWIDE

Asian Rice-Fish Systems: In parts of Southeast Asia, fish are raised in rice paddies. The fish reduce aquatic pests and their waste provides nutrients for the rice.

African Maize-Legume Systems: In several African countries, maize is intercropped with legumes like groundnuts or soybeans, enhancing soil fertility and dietary protein intake.

European Agroforestry Models: In parts of Europe, timber or fruit trees are combined with crops. The trees provide long-term income, while annual crops give short-term returns.

FUTURE PERSPECTIVES ON INTERCROPPING

Climate Resilience: As climate patterns become unpredictable, intercropping can offer resilience by diversifying crops, making fields less susceptible to specific climatic threats.

Urban and Peri-Urban Agriculture: With urbanization on the rise, space will become a limiting factor. Intercropping can be an ideal solution for urban farmers aiming to maximize produce in limited areas.

Research and Education: As the importance of sustainable agriculture grows, research institutions are focusing more on perfecting intercropping techniques and educating farmers about their benefits.

By harnessing the power of plants' synergistic relationships, intercropping stands as a testament to nature's balance. For the modern farm owner, especially those with limited space, understanding and implementing these principles can lead to enhanced productivity, sustainability, and profitability. As the world leans towards more ecologically friendly farming practices, intercropping will undoubtedly play a significant role in shaping the future of agriculture.

PLANTS THAT GROW WELL TOGETHER

UNDERSTANDING PLANT COMPANION RELATIONSHIPS

Symbiotic Relationships: Plants, like all living organisms, often engage in mutualistic interactions where both parties benefit. Such interactions can lead to enhanced growth, pest deterrence, or improved soil health.

Plant Allelopathy: Certain plants release chemicals, either from their roots or decaying leaves, that can inhibit or promote the growth of neighboring plants.

Spatial Considerations: In limited spaces, understanding which plants have complementary spatial needs (e.g., shallow versus deep roots) can maximize yield and growth.

CLASSIC COMPANION PLANTING PAIRS

Tomatoes and Basil: Basil deters pests that are harmful to tomatoes and may enhance the flavor of the adjacent tomatoes.

Corn, Beans, and Squash: Also known as the "Three Sisters," this trio supports each other. Beans climb the corn stalks and fix nitrogen, benefiting the corn and squash. The squash, with its broad leaves, suppresses weeds.

Carrots and Onions: The pungent aroma of onions masks the scent of carrots, deterring carrot flies.

BENEFITS OF COMPANION PLANTING

Pest Control: Certain plants can act as repellents or attract beneficial insects that can keep harmful pests at bay.

Soil Health and Fertility: Leguminous plants, like beans and peas, fix atmospheric nitrogen, which can benefit their companion plants by enriching the soil.

Efficient Resource Use: Complementary root depths can ensure that water and nutrients are taken from different levels of the soil, reducing competition.

CONSIDERATIONS FOR PAIRING PLANTS

Growth Patterns: It's essential to pair plants with similar growth requirements but different growth habits. This ensures they don't compete for the same space.

Nutrient Requirements: Plants with different nutritional needs can be grown together so that they don't compete for the same nutrients.

Water Requirements: Pairing plants with similar water needs can make irrigation more straightforward and efficient.

PLANTS TO AVOID GROWING TOGETHER

Tomatoes and Potatoes: Both are susceptible to the same blight, so growing them together increases the risk of disease transmission.

Beans and Garlic: Garlic can inhibit the growth of beans and other legumes.

Carrots and Dill: Dill can hinder carrot growth, so they should be planted separately.

BENEFICIAL FLOWER AND VEGETABLE PAIRINGS

Marigolds with Almost Any Vegetable: Marigolds repel nematodes and other pests, making them a great companion for various vegetables.

Nasturtiums and Cabbage: Nasturtiums deter a variety of pests, including whiteflies and cabbage loopers.

Borage and Tomatoes: Borage deters tomato hornworm and can also improve the flavor and growth of tomatoes.

UTILIZING HERBS IN COMPANION PLANTING

Rosemary and Beans: Rosemary repels bean beetles and can be a beneficial neighbor for beans.

Mint and Brassicas (like Broccoli, Cabbage): Mint deters cabbage moths and can be planted around brassicas to protect them.

Dill and Cucumbers: Dill attracts beneficial predators that can protect cucumbers from harmful pests.

FRUIT TREE COMPANIONS

Apples and Chives: Chives can help repel apple scab, a common disease in apple trees.

Strawberries and Borage: Borage can deter pests that attack strawberries and can also enhance their flavor.

Grapes and Hyssop: Hyssop can repel grape moths and can be planted around grapevines for protection.

ROLE OF GROUND COVERS AND LIVING MULCHES

White Clover: Acts as a living mulch, suppressing weeds and fixing nitrogen.

Sweet Alyssum: Attracts beneficial insects and acts as a living mulch, retaining soil moisture.

Thyme: Creates a fragrant ground cover that can deter pests and prevent weed growth.

IMPLEMENTING POLYCULTURES IN SMALL SPACES

Keyhole Gardens: These are densely planted beds, maximizing space utilization and often incorporating companion planting principles.

Vertical Stacking: Using trellises or other vertical supports, one can grow vining plants above shorter plants, effectively using vertical space.

Successional Planting: Once a crop is harvested, a complementary plant is immediately sown or planted in its place, ensuring continuous and efficient use of space.

ADVANCED COMPANION STRATEGIES

Trap Cropping: Using plants to attract pests away from main crops. For instance, planting nasturtiums around vegetables can lure aphids away, protecting the primary crops.

Nurse Cropping: Tall or robust plants protect more delicate plants from harsh conditions. For instance, sunflowers can act as a windbreak for tender plants.

Break Crops: Certain plants can be grown to break disease cycles. For example, growing a non-host crop for a season can reduce soil-borne diseases for subsequent crops.

CHALLENGES AND MISCONCEPTIONS

Over-reliance on Companion Planting: While beneficial, companion planting isn't a magic solution. Integrated pest and disease management should still be employed.

Overcrowding: In an eagerness to maximize companionship benefits, one might plant too densely, leading to competition and reduced airflow.

Lack of Research: While many companion plantings are based on anecdotal evidence, scientific research on the topic is still growing.

ONGOING RESEARCH AND FUTURE DIRECTIONS

Data-Driven Decisions: With advancements in technology, farm owners can employ sensors and software to monitor plant health and interactions, making informed decisions about companion planting.

Biodynamic Farming: This holistic approach considers the farm as an interconnected system, and companion planting plays a significant role in this methodology.

Urban Farming and Microgardens: As urban agriculture becomes more popular, understanding beneficial plant interactions becomes crucial to maximize yield in limited spaces.

Companion planting is both an art and science, representing centuries of observational knowledge combined with modern research. For the contemporary farm owner, especially one with limited space, the ability to harness these natural synergies can result in healthier crops, reduced reliance on chemical inputs, and ultimately, higher yields. By understanding and implementing the principles of beneficial plant interactions, farmers can move a step closer to sustainable and resilient agricultural systems.

CHAPTER 5

HARVESTING AND PRESERVATION

HARVESTING TECHNIQUES TO ENSURE

UNDERSTANDING PLANT MATURITY

Indicators of Maturity: Every crop has distinct signs indicating it's ready for harvest. Whether it's the color, size, texture, or aroma, these cues are essential in ensuring peak freshness and flavor. For instance, tomatoes are best harvested when they achieve a deep, uniform color, while cucumbers are picked before they get too large and seeds become hard.

Monitoring Growth Phases: Regularly inspecting the crops and comparing their growth stages with standard maturity indicators can guide the timing of the harvest.

MANUAL HARVESTING TECHNIQUES

Hand-picking: Many fruits and vegetables, like berries, tomatoes, and bell peppers, benefit from hand-picking. It minimizes damage and allows for selective harvesting, ensuring only ripe produce is gathered.

Cutting: Leafy greens, herbs, and many root crops require cutting. Using sharp tools minimizes plant stress and reduces the chances of disease.

Digging and Uprooting: For underground crops like potatoes, carrots, and onions, careful digging or uprooting is necessary to prevent damage to the produce.

MECHANICAL HARVESTING

While small-scale farms often rely on manual labor, larger operations might benefit from mechanical harvesting. Equipment, when used correctly, can ensure freshness by rapidly and efficiently harvesting produce at its peak.

Combine Harvesters: Used primarily for grains, these machines can reap, thresh, and winnow in one operation.

Specialty Harvesters: There are machines tailored for specific crops, like potato harvesters or nut shakers.

Adjusting Settings: It's crucial to adjust machinery settings to the specific crop and its maturity level to minimize damage and ensure optimal freshness.

IMMEDIATE POST-HARVEST HANDLING

Field Cooling: Crops like lettuce and broccoli benefit from rapid cooling after harvesting. Techniques include hydro-cooling (immersion in cold water) or vacuum cooling.

Shade and Cover: Produce, once harvested, should be immediately moved to a shaded area or covered to protect it from direct sunlight, reducing wilting and loss of freshness.

Handling with Care: Even the most resilient produce can get bruised. Always handle harvested crops gently. Tools like padded containers, conveyors, or soft drop points can help.

CLEANING AND GRADING

Washing: Many crops require washing to remove soil, pests, or residues. The water should be fresh and clean, with regular changes to prevent cross-contamination.

Grading: Classifying produce based on size, weight, or appearance can streamline the packaging process and ensure uniform quality.

Drying: Post-wash, it's essential to dry the produce, especially if it's to be stored. Proper drying prevents mold growth and other moisture-related issues.

STORAGE TECHNIQUES TO RETAIN FRESHNESS

Cold Storage: Temperature regulation can significantly impact the freshness of harvested produce. Refrigerated storage slows down the metabolic processes in crops, extending their freshness.

Modified Atmosphere Packaging (MAP): By altering the proportions of gases like oxygen, carbon dioxide, and nitrogen around the stored produce, its shelf life can be extended.

Ethylene Control: Many fruits release ethylene gas, which can hasten the ripening (and subsequent spoiling) of surrounding produce. Ensuring proper ventilation or using ethylene absorbers can help.

Humidity Control: While some crops require high humidity, others may need drier conditions. Investing in humidity control systems within storage can be beneficial.

SHORT-TERM VS. LONG-TERM PRESERVATION

Fresh Market Sales: For produce meant for immediate sale, the focus should be on rapid transportation to markets, ensuring it reaches consumers in its freshest state.

Long-Term Storage: For crops meant for extended storage or off-season sales, more in-depth preservation methods, like canning, freezing, or pickling, may be necessary.

RECORD KEEPING AND CONTINUOUS LEARNING

Documenting Harvest Times: Maintaining a record of when specific crops were harvested can provide insights for future harvests, enabling adjustments for better results.

Feedback Loop: Engaging with end consumers or retailers provides valuable feedback. If a particular batch of produce wasn't up to mark in terms of freshness, it's an opportunity to investigate and refine harvesting techniques.

Maintaining freshness from the moment crops are harvested until they reach the consumer is a detailed process that requires vigilance, understanding, and a commitment to best practices. As a modern farm owner, integrating these techniques ensures that the fruits of labor are enjoyed in their prime state, leading to higher consumer satisfaction and optimizing returns on investment. The techniques mentioned here aren't exhaustive but provide a strong foundational understanding of the importance of harvesting for freshness.

SEED SELECTION AND PRESERVATION

THE IMPORTANCE OF SEED SELECTION

Genetic Potential: The seed is the foundation of any crop. The quality, yield, and resilience of your produce are, in large part, determined by the genetic potential embedded in the seeds you plant.

Meeting Market Demands: Selecting the right seeds also involves understanding market trends. Are consumers in your region looking for a particular type of tomato? Is there a rising demand for non-GMO crops? Seed selection can align farm production with market demand.

Resilience to Environmental Conditions: Different seeds have varying degrees of resistance to diseases, pests, and climatic conditions. By selecting seeds adapted to your specific region and its challenges, you enhance the likelihood of a successful harvest.

SEED VARIETIES AND THEIR TRAITS

Heirloom Seeds: These are traditional varieties, passed down through generations, and often revered for their flavor and adaptability to local conditions. They're open-pollinated, meaning they reproduce true-to-type year after year.

Hybrid Seeds: These result from cross-pollinating two different parent plants. Hybrids often exhibit better disease resistance, yield, and uniformity than their parents. However, they don't usually reproduce true-to-type, making saving seeds from hybrid crops unreliable for consistent results.

Genetically Modified (GMO) Seeds: These are modified in a laboratory to exhibit certain traits, like resistance to herbicides or certain pests. While they can offer many agricultural advantages, there's a discourse around their environmental and health impacts.

SOURCING QUALITY SEEDS

Reputable Seed Suppliers: Whether purchasing seeds locally or online, always opt for well-reviewed, reputable suppliers. They can provide insights into the seed's origin, genetic traits, and growing recommendations.

Seed Exchanges: Local farming communities often organize seed exchange events. These platforms can be invaluable for obtaining locally adapted varieties and heirlooms.

Self-Harvesting: By selecting the healthiest plants in your crop to harvest seeds from, you're essentially selecting traits that you wish to perpetuate in subsequent crops.

HARVESTING SEEDS

Optimal Harvest Time: Each plant has a specific window when seeds reach their peak maturity. For instance, tomato seeds are best harvested when the fruit is ripe, whereas lettuce seeds should be collected after the plant has bolted and flowered.

Extracting and Cleaning: Once harvested, seeds often come with pulp (as in tomatoes) or chaff (as in grains). Methods like fermentation, winnowing, or simple washing can help in separating seeds from unwanted material.

Drying: It's crucial to dry seeds adequately before storage. Lay seeds out in a cool, shaded area with good airflow. Turning them occasionally ensures even drying.

SEED STORAGE

Ideal Storage Conditions: Seeds preserve best in cool, dark, and dry conditions. Moisture and warmth can trigger premature germination or seed decay.

Packaging: Using airtight containers, like glass jars with tight-sealing lids or vacuum-sealed pouches, can extend seed viability. Desiccants, like silica gel, can be added to absorb any residual moisture.

Labeling: Always label stored seeds with the variety name and date of harvest. Over time, seeds lose viability, and a well-labeled inventory helps in keeping track.

SEED VIABILITY AND GERMINATION TESTS

Viability Test: If seeds have been stored for a long time, a simple viability test can be done. Moisten a paper towel, place a few seeds on it, fold, and keep in a warm place. If most seeds sprout in a week or so, they're viable.

Regular Rotation: For optimal results, seeds should be used within their recommended viability period. Regularly rotate stored seeds, using older seeds first.

SEED PRESERVATION FOR GENETIC DIVERSITY

Importance of Diversity: Genetic diversity ensures crops can withstand various challenges. Relying on a single seed variety can make the entire crop vulnerable to a particular disease or pest.

Participate in Seed Banks: Seed banks collect, store, and distribute plant seeds, safeguarding genetic diversity. By contributing to or utilizing seed banks, farmers can play a role in conserving agricultural heritage.

REGULATORY AND ETHICAL CONSIDERATIONS

Intellectual Property Rights: Some modern seeds are patented. Using such seeds without authorization, especially for commercial purposes, can lead to legal complications.

Ethical Choices: Considering the ecological and socio-economic impacts of seed choices is crucial. Supporting organic, non-GMO, and heirloom seed initiatives can align farming practices with broader sustainability goals.

Seed selection and preservation is both a science and an art. As modern farm owners, understanding the intricacies of seeds can have profound implications for crop success, farm profitability, and the broader agricultural ecosystem. This chapter offers a roadmap to navigate the complexities of seeds, from selection to preservation, ensuring the farm's legacy thrives for generations to come.

PRESERVATION METHODS: DRYING, CANNING, FREEZING

THE IMPERATIVE OF FOOD PRESERVATION

Preservation is vital for extending the shelf life of harvests, maximizing the return on investment, and ensuring that produce is available year-round. The methods of preservation not only retain the nutritional value and flavor of the produce but also safeguard it from spoilage organisms such as bacteria, yeast, and fungi.

DRYING: THE OLDEST FORM OF PRESERVATION

Principles of Drying: Drying, fundamentally, involves removing moisture from produce. This dehydration process inhibits the growth of spoilage organisms, as they require moisture to thrive.

Sun and Air Drying: Ideal for areas with consistent sunlight and low humidity. Thinly sliced produce is spread out in the sun, with regular turning for even drying. This method is commonly used for herbs, fruits like apricots, and chilies.

Oven and Dehydrator Drying: These controlled methods are more efficient than sun drying. Ovens and electric dehydrators circulate hot air around the produce, ensuring even drying and preventing spoilage.

Vacuum and Freeze Drying: Here, produce is frozen and then placed in a vacuum chamber where moisture sublimates directly from ice to vapor. This method is highly effective in preserving the shape, color, and nutritional value of the produce.

Storing Dried Produce: Dried produce should be stored in cool, dark, and airtight containers to prevent moisture reabsorption and maximize shelf life.

CANNING: SEALING PRODUCE IN GLASS JARS

Basics of Canning: Canning involves placing produce in jars and then heating them to a temperature that destroys spoilage organisms. As the jars cool, a vacuum seal forms, preventing the entry of new organisms.

Water Bath Canning: Ideal for high-acid foods like fruits, pickles, and jams. Jars are submerged in boiling water for a specified duration, effectively sterilizing their contents.

Pressure Canning: Used for low-acid foods like vegetables and meats. A pressure canner is necessary to reach the higher temperatures required to safely preserve these foods.

Quality of Canning Jars: Always use jars designed for canning. Regularly inspect them for cracks, chips, or imperfections that might compromise the vacuum seal.

Shelf Life and Storage: Canned goods should be stored in a cool, dark place. While the sealing process extends shelf life significantly, it's recommended to consume canned produce within a year for optimal quality.

FREEZING: THE COLD STORAGE METHOD

Fundamentals of Freezing: Freezing preserves produce by halting the activity of spoilage organisms and enzymatic reactions. It's one of the most effective methods to retain the texture, flavor, and nutritional value of the harvest.

Preparing Produce for Freezing: Most vegetables benefit from blanching before freezing. This brief immersion in boiling water halts enzyme activity, ensuring the produce retains its color and flavor.

Vacuum Sealing: Removing air from the packaging prevents freezer burn and retains product quality. Vacuum sealers are an investment that pays off in preserving produce quality during extended freezing.

Optimal Freezer Temperatures: Maintain a consistent temperature of at least -18°C (0°F). Fluctuating temperatures can compromise the quality of the frozen produce.

Freezing Fruits: Fruits, unlike many vegetables, don't require blanching. However, treating them with ascorbic acid or fruit-preserving powders can prevent discoloration.

Shelf Life Considerations: While freezing extends the life of produce, it doesn't stop it from eventually deteriorating. Most fruits and vegetables maintain peak quality for about 9-12 months in the freezer.

SYNERGIES AMONG PRESERVATION METHODS

In many instances, a combination of methods is used. For instance, sun-dried tomatoes might be stored in olive oil in jars, or fruits might be dried and then frozen. Recognizing the strengths and limitations of each method allows for effective combinations that maximize shelf life and quality.

QUALITY CONTROL IN PRESERVATION

Monitoring for Spoilage: Regularly inspect preserved goods. Signs of spoilage include mold growth, off-odors, bulging can lids, or discoloration.

Ensuring Sterility: Especially in canning, it's crucial to ensure that all equipment and jars are sterile. This avoids introducing contaminants that can compromise the preservation process.

Rotation Practices: Rotate stock, using older preserved produce first. This ensures that products are always consumed within their optimal quality window.

MODERN CHALLENGES AND OPPORTUNITIES

Today's farm owner faces a unique set of challenges and opportunities in food preservation. Increased consumer awareness about additives and a preference for organic, non-GMO produce means there's a demand for clean-label preserved products. Innovations in preservation technology, combined with age-old methods, offer ways to meet these demands while maintaining profitability and sustainability.

Preserving the bounty of a harvest is a culmination of a season's hard work. Effective preservation ensures that the effort expended in planting, nurturing, and harvesting crops does not go to waste. It provides a means to enjoy the fruits of one's labor throughout the year, to hedge against future price fluctuations, and to offer consumers quality products outside the typical harvest window. As modern farm owners, mastering these preservation techniques is both a responsibility and an art.

HARVEST PRESERVATION

THE IMPORTANCE OF POST-HARVEST HANDLING

Post-harvest handling is the critical bridge between the culmination of the growing season and the consumer's plate. It encompasses all the activities that occur once a crop is harvested up to the point it's consumed, ensuring that agricultural produce maintains its freshness, nutritional quality, and safety for consumption.

Maintaining Nutritional Quality: The nutritional value of many crops starts to decline as soon as they're harvested. Proper post-harvest handling slows this degradation, preserving the vital nutrients within.

Reducing Post-Harvest Losses: Improper post-harvest handling can lead to significant losses, both in terms of quantity and quality. By implementing proper practices, a modern farm owner can avoid such losses, ensuring that a higher percentage of the produce reaches the end consumer in pristine condition.

Ensuring Food Safety: Improper handling can introduce or promote the growth of foodborne pathogens. Adopting stringent post-harvest handling protocols is paramount in preventing contamination and subsequent outbreaks of foodborne illnesses.

INITIAL POST-HARVEST HANDLING PROCEDURES

Harvest Timing: The time of day when harvesting occurs can impact the longevity and quality of produce. For instance, harvesting in the cooler hours of the early morning can reduce the field heat of certain crops, prolonging their freshness.

Gentle Handling: Bruising or damaging the produce makes it more susceptible to decay and deterioration. Using padded harvesting containers, gentle harvesting tools, and training workers can minimize this damage.

Field Cleaning: Removing soil, leaves, and other debris in the field reduces the load for subsequent cleaning processes and prevents potential contaminants from entering the processing area.

Field Cooling: For crops sensitive to field heat, rapid cooling methods like hydrocooling or forced-air cooling can be employed directly in the field or shortly after harvest.

TRANSPORTATION AND STORAGE CONSIDERATIONS

Temperature Control: Maintaining the right temperature is crucial for slowing down the metabolic processes of harvested produce. Cold storage, for instance, is vital for many fruits and vegetables.

Modified and Controlled Atmospheres: Altering the concentrations of oxygen, carbon dioxide, and other gases can slow down ripening and deterioration processes. Techniques range from simple storage in sealed containers to advanced controlled atmosphere storage facilities.

Humidity Levels: High humidity can promote fungal growth, while low humidity can cause desiccation. Balancing humidity, often alongside temperature control, is essential for many crops.

Ethylene Management: Ethylene is a natural plant hormone that can accelerate ripening. Managing its levels, either by ventilation or using ethylene scrubbers, is crucial when storing ethylene-sensitive produce.

CLEANING AND PROCESSING

Washing and Cleaning: This step removes dirt, pesticides, and potential pathogens. However, it's essential to use clean water and regularly sanitize equipment to prevent cross-contamination.

Sorting and Grading: Sorting produce based on size, maturity, and quality ensures that only the best produce reaches the consumer, enhancing marketability and fetch prices.

Packaging Considerations: The right packaging can significantly extend the shelf life of produce. Vacuum-sealed bags, for instance, can prevent the growth of aerobic bacteria. The choice of packaging material, permeability to gases, and physical protection it offers are all critical considerations.

ADVANCED PRESERVATION TECHNIQUES

Irradiation: Exposing produce to ionizing radiation can kill pathogens and insects and extend shelf life. However, its use is subject to strict regulations and consumer perceptions.

High-Pressure Processing (HPP): This non-thermal pasteurization method subjects produce to high pressures, killing microbes without the need for high temperatures, thus preserving the sensory and nutritional properties of the food.

Antimicrobial Edible Coatings: These are thin layers of edible material applied to the produce's surface, which can carry antimicrobial agents, extending shelf life and providing an additional layer of safety.

ENSURING TRACEABILITY

In the era of global food chains, being able to trace produce back to its source is essential for both accountability and safety. Implementing traceability systems, whether manual logs or advanced blockchain technologies, ensures that any issues can be rapidly identified and addressed.

CONTINUOUS MONITORING AND QUALITY ASSURANCE

Regular Inspections: Conducting routine checks on stored produce helps identify potential issues before they escalate, ensuring that quality is maintained.

Data-Driven Decisions: Modern storage facilities are equipped with sensors that monitor temperature, humidity, and other environmental factors. Analyzing this data can provide insights into optimizing storage conditions.

Staff Training: Regularly training staff in the best practices of post-harvest handling ensures that everyone is aligned in the goal of preserving the quality of the harvest.

MARKET CONSIDERATIONS

Consumer Preferences: Today's consumers are more informed and discerning. They may prefer organic produce, locally-sourced items, or those with minimal processing. Being attuned to these preferences can guide post-harvest handling decisions.

Regulatory Compliance: Different regions have varying regulations regarding post-harvest treatments, especially when it comes to additives or processes like irradiation. Ensuring compliance is essential to avoid legal complications and maintain consumer trust.

The journey of produce, from the field to the consumer, is fraught with challenges. Each step in the post-harvest process has its intricacies and requires careful consideration. But, with meticulous planning, continuous monitoring, and by leveraging modern technologies, it's entirely feasible to deliver fresh, nutritious, and safe produce to consumers, regardless of the time elapsed since harvest. As modern farm owners, the onus is on us to champion these best practices, ensuring that our hard work during the growing season translates into a bounty that stands the test of time.

BOOK 3

CHAPTER 6

REARING SMALL ANIMALS

REARING CHICKENS FOR EGGS AND MEAT

DELVING INTO THE INTRICACIES OF CHICKEN BIOLOGY AND BEHAVIOR

Chickens, beyond being an iconic symbol of the farmyard, present a world rich in biology and behavior. The key to successfully rearing them for both eggs and meat lies in understanding the nuanced details of their physiology and daily activities. Let's embark on this insightful journey.

Unfurling the Blueprint of Chicken Anatomy and Physiology

At its core, the anatomy and physiology of a chicken are marvels of nature. Their skeletal system is feather-light, a delicate blend of fused and individual bones. This composition aids in their movement and, for some, brief flight. The keel, a protruding feature of the breastbone, offers a sturdy base for their flight muscles.

But what about the process of converting feed into energy? The digestive system is an intricate pathway, starting at the beak, culminating in the cloaca. Along this journey, the crop stores food, the gizzard grinds it, and the intestines extract the essential nutrients.

Moreover, the respiratory system of chickens is a masterpiece of efficiency. With air sacs ensuring a continuous flow of air during both inhalation and exhalation, they possess a unique mechanism to oxygenate their blood. This mechanism starkly contrasts with mammals.

When it comes to reproduction, hens are a study in efficiency. With only one functional ovary, typically the left, the egg formation is a precise process taking about 25 hours. Shortly after one egg is laid, another begins its formation.

Lastly, their nervous system paints a picture of heightened senses. Their broad field of vision, almost encompassing 300 degrees, is due to their eyes' strategic lateral positioning.

The Life's Journey of Chickens

Every chicken undergoes a fascinating life journey, from a minuscule embryo in an egg to a full-fledged bird. The embryonic dance inside the egg is a 21-day process, critically dependent on optimal temperature and humidity conditions.

Post-hatching, the world meets precocial chicks with soft downy feathers. Though they exhibit early signs of independence by walking and pecking, warmth remains a non-negotiable need.

As time progresses, these chicks undergo a metamorphosis into pullets or cockerels, showcasing true feathers and increased stature. This stage eventually gives way to the laying and meat production phase, with the intricate process of molting interspersed, where they rejuvenate their feather coat.

A Dive into Chicken Behavior

Chickens, being inherently social creatures, operate on a structured hierarchical system or the "pecking order." This social ladder determines access to food, water, and the best nesting spots.

Their daily activities paint a picture of nature's routine. The act of foraging, where they diligently search for seeds and insects, stands testament to their natural dietary instincts. Dust bathing is another therapeutic ritual, ensuring feather health and ridding them of external parasites.

As night descends, chickens seek the safety and comfort of elevated roosts. Occasionally, a strong maternal instinct engulfs certain hens. Known as broodiness, they display an intense desire to incubate and hatch eggs.

Balancing Nutrition and Diet

Nutritional balance is the linchpin of healthy chicken rearing. Carbohydrates, proteins, fats, and a slew of vitamins and minerals play their part at various life stages. Commercial feeds cater to these stages, but a judicious mix of supplemental greens, fruits, and grains enhances their diet. And of course, the lifeblood of their diet—water—must be pure, plentiful, and ever-present.

Steering Through Health Challenges

As with all livestock, health management for chickens pivots on prevention. Biosecurity measures, vaccinations, and regular health checks form the trinity of proactive care. Early signs of distress, like lethargy or changes in egg production, can signal potential health issues, warranting immediate attention.

Deciphering Breeds and Genetics

The world of chicken breeds is vast, spanning heritage breeds that harken back to traditional farming days and modern hybrid breeds optimized for contemporary needs. For the discerning farmer, there's also the art and science of selective breeding, refining specific desired traits within a flock.

The world of chickens, their biology, and behavior is a tapestry of interwoven intricacies. For the modern farm owner, understanding these details is instrumental in ensuring the birds' welfare while optimizing their egg and meat production.

CRAFTING THE PERFECT HOME FOR YOUR FLOCK

When it comes to rearing chickens, the housing you provide plays a vital role in ensuring their health and productivity. Here's what you need to know about setting up a comfortable and secure environment for your flock:

Safety First: Whether you're building a coop from scratch or buying one pre-made, the security of your chickens should be top priority. It's essential to have sturdy wire mesh around windows and the base of the coop to deter any potential predators. Doors should be lockable, and if you've got an outdoor run, consider overhead netting to protect against birds of prey.

Breathing Easy: A well-ventilated coop ensures your chickens get plenty of fresh air, which is crucial for their well-being. This setup also helps keep moisture, dust, and ammonia at bay. Ideally, vents should be positioned high up to let out hot air and moisture, but it's useful if they can be adjusted according to the weather.

Bracing for Weather: If you live in a place with extreme temperatures, insulation is a must. In the colder months, you can use heat lamps or heating plates to keep your chickens warm – just ensure they're installed safely. On the hotter days, shade and good airflow are key.

Let There Be Light: Chickens thrive in natural light. It boosts their growth and ensures steady egg production. But during shorter winter days, you might need to add some supplemental lighting.

Space Matters: The amount of room your chickens have can significantly impact their happiness and productivity. A general rule of thumb is 2-3 square feet per bird in the coop, with 8-10 square feet in an outdoor run.

Housing Options: Your choices range from mobile chicken coops, which are fantastic for rotating foraging areas, to stationary coops, which are more permanent and often paired with an outdoor run. There are also multi-tiered systems, perfect for maximizing space, and free-range systems that offer birds large outdoor areas.

Inside the Coop: Roosting bars are a must, offering chickens a comfortable elevated spot to sleep. Nesting boxes give hens a private area for laying, and you'll need approximately one box for every 4-5 hens. Don't forget the litter and bedding to keep things clean, and ensure feeders and waterers are accessible to all birds.

Exploring the Outdoors: If your chickens have an outdoor space, ensure it's safe with appropriate fencing. Incorporate dust-bathing areas for their feather maintenance, and provide shade and shelter to encourage outdoor activities. Consider growing plants or herbs for them to forage.

Keep It Clean: Consistent maintenance and cleanliness can't be emphasized enough. Regularly inspect the coop, establish a cleaning routine, and prepare for seasonal changes. Also, ensure you have measures in place for pest and rodent control.

A well-thought-out housing system can significantly impact the welfare of your chickens. By catering to their needs, you not only ensure their well-being but also guarantee better quality eggs and meat. It's a win-win for both the birds and their caretakers.

CHICKEN NUTRITION AND FEEDING

Raising healthy chickens requires a solid grasp of their nutritional needs. Just as humans need a balanced diet, chickens too thrive when given the right mix of nutrients. Here's a comprehensive guide on what, when, and how to feed your flock.

What Chickens Need:

Macronutrients:

☐ **Proteins:** These are vital for their growth, egg production, and the development of feathers. Common sources are soybean meal, canola meal, and various animal by-products.

☐ **Carbohydrates:** Chickens derive their energy mainly from grains such as corn, wheat, and barley.

☐ **Fats:** These offer a concentrated burst of energy and are found in grains, with some feeds having additional fats or oils.

Micronutrients:

☐ **Vitamins:** These play roles in many physiological functions. Chickens need both fat-soluble (A, D, E, and K) and water-soluble vitamins (B complex and vitamin C).

☐ **Minerals:** Important for bone health, blood clotting, and other processes. This includes macrominerals like calcium and phosphorus, as well as trace minerals like zinc and iodine.

☐ **Water:** Often overlooked but water is the most crucial. It aids digestion, regulates body temperature, and supports metabolic processes.

Choosing the Right Feed:

☐ **Starter Feed:** Best for chicks, this has a high protein content, supporting their rapid growth from hatching up to 6-8 weeks.

☐ **Grower Feed:** This is the next step from starter feed, meant for birds from 6-8 weeks until they're almost ready to lay eggs or for slaughter.

☐ **Layer Feed:** For hens that are laying eggs, this feed contains increased calcium for robust eggshells.

☐ **Broiler and Finisher Feeds:** These are designed for meat birds. The formulations cater to their rapid growth requirements and optimize meat yield and quality.

☐ **Specialty Feeds:** These are tailored for specific needs, such as supporting hens during molting or aiding those with eggshell issues.

Feeding Approaches:

☐ **Free-Choice:** The feed is always available. It's commonly used for layers, ensuring a steady egg production.

- **Restricted Feeding:** Here, set amounts are given at specific times, often employed for broilers to manage their growth and avoid health complications.

- **Phase Feeding:** This approach adjusts the feed based on the chicken's life stage, ensuring they get what they need without excess or deficiency.

- **Foraging and Supplementary:** This involves allowing chickens to roam, graze, and eat natural food sources, or supplementing their diet with scratch grains and fresh produce.

Deciphering Feed Labels:

- **Ingredient List:** This tells you what's in the feed, listed typically in descending order by weight.

- **Guaranteed Analysis:** This section offers information on the key nutrients in the feed.

- **Feeding Instructions:** A guide on how much to feed based on the chicken's purpose and stage of life.

Storing Feed:

- **Storage:** Using containers with tight lids and keeping feed in a dry, cool place preserves its quality.

- **Rotation:** Always use older feed before the new stock.

- **Quality Checks:** Inspect feed for signs of mold, pests, or spoilage, discarding anything that seems off.

Water Management:

Water intake for chickens is typically double their feed consumption. Ensure they have a continuous clean supply, with waterers cleaned regularly and positioned to minimize contamination.

Adapting to Unique Situations:

Whether it's managing molting, dealing with stress, or adhering to specialized diets like organic or non-GMO, understanding the nuances of chicken nutrition helps in adjusting their diet accordingly.

The right nutrition is paramount for the health and productivity of chickens. Being informed and attentive to their dietary needs ensures not only their well-being but also the quality of their produce, be it meat or eggs. It's a blend of science and care that leads to a successful poultry venture.

POULTRY HEALTH AND DISEASE MANAGEMENT

To run a successful poultry farm, understanding the health and wellbeing of your chickens is paramount. Here's an in-depth look into maintaining chicken health and addressing any issues that arise.

Core Tenets of Poultry Health:

- **Prevention is Key:** Before problems arise, prioritize proactive management. Regular health checks and ongoing surveillance can go a long way in minimizing potential outbreaks and reducing associated costs.

- **Biosecurity:** Think of this as the frontline defense against diseases. Limit and monitor access to your farm, uphold strict cleanliness standards, and always quarantine new additions to the flock.

- **Vaccination:** Protect your flock from widespread diseases through a well-structured vaccination program. This shields them from prevalent threats and fortifies the health of the entire flock.

Spotting Health Red Flags:

- **Behavioral Shifts:** Noticeable changes, be it reduced activity or alterations in social dynamics, can hint at potential health concerns.

- **Physical Indicators:** Look out for symptoms like unkempt feathers, discolored combs, or unusual discharges. Such signs often signify underlying ailments.

- **Production Fluctuations:** Be alarmed if there's a sudden drop in egg output, slowed weight gain, or an uptick in deaths.

Navigating Common Ailments:

From the notorious Avian Influenza and Newcastle Disease to conditions like Infectious Bronchitis and Coccidiosis, it's vital to know their symptoms and preventive measures. Vaccination, combined with biosecurity, often stands as the primary defense.

Battling Parasites:

- **Ward off Internal Parasites:** Regular deworming, informed by fecal tests, can nip worm infestations in the bud. Hygiene, coupled with smart grazing strategies, can further reduce risks.

- **Tackle External Threats:** Keep a watchful eye for mites, lice, and fleas. Routine checks, spotless coops, and timely treatments can keep such pests at bay.

Addressing Diet-Driven Problems:

From issues like egg-binding due to calcium shortages to conditions like fatty liver syndrome or rickets, addressing nutritional imbalances is crucial. Often, tweaking the diet or introducing supplements can rectify these issues.

Environment-Induced Challenges:

Whether it's the stifling heat or biting cold, environmental stressors can weigh heavily on poultry health. Provide ample ventilation, ensure access to cool water, and create a sheltered environment to combat these challenges.

Medicinal Measures:

While antibiotics remain a potent tool, judicious use is essential to sidestep resistance. Complement this with natural remedies like herbs and probiotics that bolster health. During crises, like heatwaves or disease outbreaks, electrolyte supplements can prove invaluable.

Keeping Tabs:

Regular health examinations and meticulous record-keeping, detailing everything from vaccination dates to treatment histories, are indispensable. In instances of unexpected deaths, consider necropsies to determine the root cause.

A Collaborative Endeavor:

Foster ties with poultry vets for expert guidance. Ensure that your farm staff remains up-to-date with the latest in biosecurity and disease recognition. And remember, there's strength in numbers—partnering with the broader farming community can amplify collective knowledge and resilience.

The health of your flock directly influences the prosperity of your poultry venture. By being vigilant, proactive, and informed, you not only safeguard your chickens but also ensure the longevity and profitability of your enterprise.

THE ART OF EGG PRODUCTION

Egg production is a delicate balance of science, nature, and care. Here's an in-depth journey through the world of egg farming.

Selecting the Right Breed:

From the highly efficient White Leghorns known for their white eggs to the versatile Rhode Island Reds with their brown eggs, breed selection is crucial. Some farmers lean towards heritage breeds like Sussex or Orpingtons, valuing their resilience and unique behaviors. Then, there are hybrid layers, like the Golden Comet, bred specifically for abundant egg yields and disease resistance.

Understanding the Laying Rhythm:

Hens usually commence their laying journey at 5-6 months. They swiftly reach a zenith, laying almost daily. But nature has its cycles – a year in, production tapers off, and hens might undergo moulting, a phase of shedding and regenerating feathers. Post-moult, they're back in the game, albeit at a slightly diminished pace.

Factors that Pull the Strings:

- **Diet Matters:** Optimal egg output demands a diet abundant in proteins, calcium for sturdy shells, and vital vitamins.

- **Let There be Light:** Around 14-16 hours of it daily, in fact. Artificial lighting can be a savior during shorter days.

- **Keep Calm and Lay On:** Stress, be it due to a prowling predator or abrupt environmental shifts, can hamper production.

- **The Health Quotient:** Unaddressed ailments can play spoilsport, causing a sharp drop in egg numbers.

The Quality Factor:

Eggshells reflect calcium intake, the hen's age, and possible diseases. The yolk's hue? It's all about the diet. And as hens mature, they grace us with slightly larger eggs.

Handling with Care:

Collect your eggy treasures daily – more often in sweltering climates or during laying highs. While cleaning, a gentle brush should do for minor dirt. However, be cautious when washing since it can strip away the egg's protective layer. And remember, cooler storage conditions extend freshness.

From Eggs to Chicks:

If hatching is on your agenda, pick the cream of the crop: spotless, well-shaped eggs. During incubation, consistency is key – 37.5°C (99.5°F) and 55-60% humidity. And don't forget to turn the eggs, ensuring even embryo growth.

Crunching the Numbers:

Factor in every cost, from feed to infrastructure, to gauge the actual cost per egg. Pricing should reflect these costs, market trends, and any specialty aspects, like organic rearing. And diversifying? Think pasteurized eggs, unique recipes, or even bakery delights.

Overcoming Hurdles:

Safeguard your flock from predators with secure housing. Ward off diseases like Avian Influenza through biosecurity measures, regular checks, and timely vaccinations. Stay vigilant for parasites and adapt housing to tackle weather extremes.

Ethics and Eggs:

The debate between cage-free and caged is pivotal, with a growing demand for humane practices that allow natural behaviors. Forcing hens into molting through starvation is frowned upon. Gentle handling and genuine care go a long way.

In the evolving world of egg production, adapting to modern techniques while prioritizing ethical considerations ensures not just a plentiful yield but also meets the discerning demands of today's consumers. Dedication to learning and a heartfelt commitment to poultry welfare is the golden recipe for success in this sphere.

REARING MEAT CHICKENS

In the realm of poultry farming, rearing chickens for meat is a meticulous practice that demands keen insight into the chicken's lifecycle, nutrition, and living conditions. The ultimate goal is to produce meat that's of high quality, both in terms of taste and ethical standards.

Breeds Suitable for Meat Production

When selecting breeds for meat production, there are several contenders. Broilers, like the Cornish Cross, are renowned for their rapid growth and generous breast meat, making them a popular choice. The Red Ranger, while growing at a slower pace, is celebrated for its active foraging behavior and superior meat flavor. Dual-purpose breeds, such as the Rhode Island Red and Plymouth Rock, strike a balance between egg production and meat yield. Heritage breeds, like the Delaware, though slower-growing, are treasured for the richness of their meat, a testament to traditional poultry farming.

The Initial Stages: Brooding Period

The brooding period is crucial for meat chickens. During this time, the environment should be warm and free from drafts, which can be achieved using heat lamps or radiant heat plates. The chicks should be introduced to a high-protein starter feed and given unlimited access to fresh water. It's also essential to gradually reduce the heat each week, helping them acclimate to regular temperatures as they mature.

Growing Out Period

As chicks grow, their nutritional needs evolve. Around the 3-4 week mark, they should transition to a grower feed, which is slightly lower in protein but continues to support steady growth. Given their rapid growth rate, meat birds also demand more space, both inside the coop and in any outdoor spaces they can access. Regular weight checks can ensure they are growing at the expected rate.

Nutrition Essentials

Nutrition plays a pivotal role in rearing meat chickens. The feed regimen typically follows a sequence: starting with a high-protein starter, transitioning to a balanced grower feed, and concluding with a finisher feed to optimize meat quality in the weeks leading up to processing. For those keen on organic production, it's imperative to select feeds that are certified organic and devoid of genetically modified organisms. Additional supplements, like grit or probiotics, can further enhance digestion and overall gut health.

Housing and Lifestyle Considerations

The debate between free-range and confined rearing is ongoing. Free-range chickens benefit from natural pastures, supplementing their diet, and engaging in instinctual behaviors. The practice of using "chicken tractors" or mobile coops can also be advantageous, allowing birds to access fresh pasture regularly and enrich the soil with their droppings. While confined rearing might lead to faster growth, it does raise certain welfare concerns.

Health Management

Maintaining the health of meat chickens involves proactive measures. Consider vaccines to safeguard against common poultry ailments and perform regular inspections for external parasites. Any signs of illness, from lethargy to respiratory distress, should be addressed promptly to prevent widespread outbreaks.

Processing Meat Birds

The age for processing varies depending on the breed and desired meat quality, but most broilers are ready between 6-8 weeks. The processing phase requires specialized equipment and a comprehensive understanding of local regulations. Whether selling the meat fresh or frozen, maintaining appropriate storage temperatures is paramount.

Ethical Considerations

Today's consumers are increasingly aware of animal welfare and sustainable farming practices. As a farm owner, ensuring that birds live in clean, spacious conditions and are protected from predators is non-negotiable. When it comes to processing, adopt methods that minimize distress. Additionally, consider implementing practices that are environmentally friendly, such as rotational grazing or using organic feed.

Rearing meat chickens is a nuanced endeavor that marries science with ethics. The rewards, both in terms of economic gains and the satisfaction of producing high-quality, ethically raised meat, are worth the effort and dedication the process demands.

ETHICAL AND HUMANE MANAGEMENT IN MODERN POULTRY FARMING

In the ever-evolving world of poultry farming, understanding and respecting the ethical obligations to the animals under our care is of utmost importance. Recognizing chickens as sentient beings with unique needs, emotions, and complex behaviors adds depth to this responsibility. Modern research affirms that chickens can experience a myriad of emotions, pain, and stress. This heightened understanding of their sentience challenges us to balance productivity with their welfare, ensuring both healthy yields and their overall well-being.

The living conditions we provide for chickens directly influence their health and happiness. Free-range systems, for instance, offer a more natural environment where chickens can access the outdoors, engage in dust baths, forage, and display other instinctive behaviors. While these systems require vigilant maintenance to ensure safety from potential threats like predators and diseases, they greatly enhance the quality of life for the birds. On the other hand, barn-raised or cage-free systems, although indoors, ensure chickens aren't confined and can move freely. For farms transitioning from traditional methods, enriched cages provide a middle-ground solution, allowing birds more space than conventional cages but less than free-range conditions.

Equally important to their living environment is their diet. The nutritional needs of chickens vary based on factors like age, breed, and purpose—whether they're layers or broilers. Key to their diet are essential proteins, vitamins, minerals, and other energy sources. Additionally, continuous access to clean, fresh water is crucial for their digestion and metabolism. Ethical farming also takes a strong stance against non-therapeutic antibiotics and growth promoters, focusing more on a balanced diet and sustainable management practices.

To ensure the flock remains in optimal health, regular health checks and vaccinations are imperative. These not only prevent outbreaks of diseases but also detect early signs of illness or stress. In line with sustainable and natural farming practices, many modern farms are exploring the use of natural remedies, including herbs, essential oils, and probiotics, to bolster immunity and enhance the overall health of the flock.

Breeding, when approached ethically, should not solely focus on productivity. It's vital to avoid extreme traits that may lead to health issues. Furthermore, ethical breeding practices should emphasize preserving genetic diversity, as a narrow genetic pool can increase susceptibility to diseases.

During their life cycle, chickens may need to be transported or handled, and it's crucial that these processes cause minimal stress. Proper training of farm staff and the thoughtful design of transport vehicles can make a significant difference in the welfare of the birds. When rearing chickens for meat, their end-of-life experience should be humane, incorporating practices like stunning before slaughter to ensure they don't experience pain.

Engaging consumers in the conversation about ethical poultry farming is equally significant. Transparency in farming practices fosters trust and allows consumers to make informed choices. By hosting farm tours, workshops, and other educational events, we can bridge the gap between producers and consumers. Additionally, farms that earn third-party certifications for ethical practices further instill confidence in their products.

The ethos of poultry farming should revolve around the principles of ethics and compassion. Prioritizing the welfare of chickens and respecting their intrinsic value allows us to elevate the industry standards, resulting in a harmonious blend of quality products and moral integrity.

ECONOMIC CONSIDERATIONS

When venturing into poultry farming, understanding the economic facets is crucial. From the initial investments to the recurrent expenses, each financial decision will shape the profitability and sustainability of the endeavor.

Starting a poultry farm involves several significant investments. The housing system is a primary concern, with costs varying based on your choice—whether it's free-range, barn-raised, or cage-free. While weighing the costs, it's important to keep in mind factors such as the size, materials, and long-term maintenance. Accompanying the housing are feeding and water systems. Automated feeders, while more costly upfront, can significantly reduce labor expenses and ensure consistency. Furthermore, if the farm's focus is eggs, investing in efficient egg collection systems can optimize productivity.

Land acquisition, a major component of initial expenses, needs careful evaluation. Factors such as accessibility, fertility, and suitability for free-ranging will play into the cost and long-term productivity. Additionally, the choice of breeding stock will dictate initial breeding expenses. It's crucial to prioritize breed quality and health.

Operational costs will become the day-to-day reality once the farm is up and running. Feed, often the most substantial expense, can be a variable cost, depending on market fluctuations. It might be worth considering bulk purchases or even exploring on-site feed production. Healthcare, encompassing vaccinations and preventative measures, is another crucial cost to anticipate. Labor, utilities like water and electricity, and other necessities will also consume a significant part of the budget.

Breed selection is pivotal for productivity. The right breed can substantially increase yields, be it for eggs or meat. Monitoring factors like the feed conversion ratio, which measures feed efficiency, can provide insights into profitability. Equally vital is keeping a close eye on mortality rates. High mortality can drastically affect profitability, but with the right preventative measures, these can be mitigated.

Sales and marketing will dictate revenue. While determining the price point, consider production costs and add a margin, factoring in any premium characteristics like organic or free-range status. Direct sales might offer higher profits, but working with distributors could simplify operations. In today's digital age, branding cannot be ignored. An online presence, attractive packaging, and consistent messaging can work wonders in building a loyal customer base.

Financial prudence requires a well-structured budget and diligent record-keeping. Detailed records assist in assessing performance and ensuring regulatory compliance. Moreover, staying informed about government subsidies or grants can offer some financial reprieve. Insurance is another area worth considering, offering protection against unforeseen events.

Sustainable practices can also bring economic benefits. Renewable energy sources like solar panels might involve an initial investment but can reduce long-term utility costs. Similarly, organic farming practices, while potentially more expensive at the outset, can command higher market prices, balancing the scales.

A commitment to research and development will keep the farm at the forefront of the industry. This, combined with regular training for staff, can optimize efficiency. As profits start rolling in, expansion can be the next logical step, amplifying production capacity.

The economics of poultry farming is a complex interplay of investments, operational costs, sales, and long-term strategic decisions. By staying informed and making judicious choices, poultry farm owners can find a balance between profitability and sustainable growth.

BREEDING AND GENETICS IN CHICKEN REARING

As one delves into the intricate world of poultry farming, the emphasis on genetics and breeding becomes undeniably clear. In shaping the characteristics and productivity of a flock, these two components hold the reins, guiding everything from the vibrant hue of feathers to the innate capability for egg-laying.

Unraveling the Complexities of Chicken Genetics

The enigma of chicken genetics isn't just academic fascination; it's the roadmap to deciphering how a flock might perform, resist illnesses, and adapt. Let's break down some pivotal terminologies:

- **Alleles** are akin to genetic variations or flavors of a gene, with every chicken being endowed with a pair, inherited from each parent.

- When a chicken's pair of alleles resonate in harmony, it's termed **Homozygous**. Conversely, when they differ, it's **Heterozygous**.

- Traits can manifest dominantly or recessively. A **dominant trait** needs just one allele to assert itself, while a **recessive one** waits for a matching pair.

Genetic Diversity: Nature's Insurance

A flock's resilience often hinges on its genetic diversity. Such diversity acts as a buffer against diseases and a flexibly adaptive force against environmental changes. Plus, it's akin to having a treasure trove of diverse traits, giving breeders ample options when they wish to emphasize certain characteristics.

Crafting Genetics: Breeding Techniques

Breeding isn't merely allowing chickens to mate; it's an art and science of orchestrating genetic symphonies.

- **Selective Breeding** is akin to curating genetics. By choosing specific chickens based on cherished traits and letting them mate, one can gradually amplify these traits within the flock. This technique branches into:

- **Line Breeding**, which focuses on amplifying traits by letting close relatives mate. However, this approach walks on a tightrope; excessive line breeding risks inbreeding complications.

- **Outcrossing**, which is like a breath of fresh genetic air, involves mating unrelated members of the same breed, merging familiar traits with new genetic material.

- Venturing into **Crossbreeding** is like blending the essences of two distinct breeds. This often births offspring that reap the benefits of hybrid vigor, showcasing superior qualities, be it in growth or productivity.

Harnessing the Power of Chicken Genomes

Recent advancements have unveiled the entire chicken genome. This revelation is not just a scientific feat but a boon for poultry farmers.

- Markers within the genome can hint at productivity. Recognizing these markers means one can make breeding decisions long before chickens mature.

- Some genes are like shields, granting resistance against specific ailments. Prioritizing these genes can cultivate a flock that's hardier against diseases.

- Adaptability isn't just behavioral; it's genetic. Certain genes thrive in specific climates, making them valuable depending on the environmental conditions of the farm.

Tailoring Breeds for Intent

Not all chickens are created equal, especially when we look at them through the lens of purpose.

- **Layers** and **Broilers** are the epitomes of genetic tailoring. Layers have genetics optimized for prolific egg production, while broilers boast genes that emphasize meat quality and growth.

- Then, there are **Heritage Breeds**, bearing ancient and unique genes, catering to niche markets with their distinct offerings, be it in resilience or aesthetics.

Stepping into Controversy: Genetically Modified Chickens

While still a debated realm, the science has explored modifying chicken genes directly to inculcate certain traits, from heightened disease resistance to modified growth rates. But venturing here demands an intricate dance around ethics, health, and market reception.

Breeding and Ethics: A Balancing Act

- A constant vigil against excessive inbreeding is vital to avoid the web of health issues it might spawn.

- While artificial insemination offers precision, natural mating preserves the natural behavior and essence of the chickens.

- Single-minded pursuit of specific traits should never overshadow holistic health and vitality.

Record-Keeping: The Backbone of Breeding

Effective breeding is as much about foresight as it is about retrospection. Detailed records, be it in pedigree charts, documented traits, or health histories, ensure that breeding decisions are grounded in data, history, and insights.

In the evolving tapestry of poultry farming, genetics and breeding are the threads weaving success stories. As we continue to deepen our understanding and techniques, these elements promise enhanced productivity, healthier flocks, and the satisfaction of meeting market demands efficiently.

NAVIGATING CHALLENGES AND AVOIDING PITFALLS

Rearing chickens, whether for eggs or meat, is a dynamic and engaging venture. However, like any endeavor, it is not without its complexities. Let's delve into some of the challenges faced by poultry farmers and the common mistakes that can occur, along with insights on how to navigate these waters adeptly.

Nutrition and Feed Choices A common oversight in poultry farming is the nutrition provided to the flock. While proteins like soybean meal or fish meal are essential, especially for laying hens and rapidly growing broilers, some farmers might not offer enough. Conversely, relying too much on energy-rich grains such as corn and wheat can lead to nutrient deficiencies. The key lies in striking a balance and ensuring chickens get vital elements like calcium for eggshell formation and grit for digestion. Furthermore, always ensure a consistent water supply; it's not just for hydration but also for nutrient absorption.

Creating the Right Environment The habitat you create for your chickens plays a pivotal role in their well-being. They need a safe haven, shielded from predators and elements like extreme temperatures. It's easy to underestimate space requirements, leading to overcrowded coops, which in turn can escalate stress and aggression among the flock. Cleanliness is another cornerstone. Without regular sanitation, you risk attracting pests and fostering a breeding ground for diseases. Moreover, good ventilation is not merely a luxury but a necessity, ensuring a fresh supply of air and the expulsion of harmful gases.

Decoding the Intricacies of Breeding Breeding can be a challenging terrain to navigate. The risk of inbreeding looms large when breeding within a closed group. This approach often produces weaker offspring, susceptible to diseases. It's also paramount to choose the right breeding pairs to ensure that the offspring inherit the desired traits, whether related to meat quality or egg-laying capabilities.

Ensuring Health and Mitigating Diseases The health of your flock is the bedrock of a successful poultry farm. Regular health checks can preempt many potential issues. The introduction of new members to the flock or the presence of a sick member demands stringent quarantine measures. A word of caution: while antibiotics are valuable tools, they should be used judiciously to prevent the rise of resistant strains. And let's not forget about parasites; regular checks and treatments are your best defense.

Understanding Chicken Behavior and Handling Chickens, though often seen merely as livestock, have intricate social structures and behaviors. Handling them requires care and patience. Rough handling can cause stress and injury. Additionally, within the flock, understanding the pecking order is essential. Severe aggression or bullying, if left unchecked, can lead to injuries.

Market Dynamics and Economic Considerations Economics can't be ignored when rearing chickens. Factors like the efficiency of feed conversion play a vital role in determining profitability. Furthermore, the market for poultry products isn't static. Staying attuned to market demands and price fluctuations will ensure that you neither overproduce nor fall short. Adhering to local regulations and considering certifications can also open doors to premium pricing.

Infrastructure and Training: The Foundations of Success Using the latest equipment can make operations smoother and more efficient. It's equally important to have backup systems, especially in areas prone to outages. Efficient waste management is not just about cleanliness; it can also offer additional revenue streams, such as selling chicken manure as fertilizer. Lastly, continuous learning and staff training are not mere checkboxes but vital components of a successful poultry farm.

In the multifaceted journey of poultry farming, knowledge is power. By staying informed and vigilant, and by addressing challenges head-on, poultry farmers can not only avoid common pitfalls but also thrive and prosper in this rewarding venture.

ADVANCED TECHNIQUES AND TECHNOLOGIES IN REARING CHICKENS

In the contemporary world of poultry farming, the fusion of advanced techniques and modern technologies is not just a trend—it's a necessary evolution. Today, the emphasis is on precision, sustainability, and efficiency, and this push is transforming the very fabric of poultry management.

Consider the rise of precision poultry farming. No longer do farmers solely rely on their instincts or traditional methods. Instead, they're adopting modern sensors that monitor environmental parameters with remarkable accuracy. These aren't just tools that sound an alarm when the temperature drops. They actively track parameters such as air quality, humidity, and even detect harmful gases like ammonia, ensuring that the flock always has the optimal environment for growth and productivity.

Now, imagine a chicken wearing a device. It might seem outlandish at first, but wearable technology for chickens is becoming increasingly common. These smart devices, often comfortably attached to a chicken's leg or wing, provide invaluable data on each bird's movement patterns. Any significant deviation might indicate health issues, allowing farmers to act proactively.

The focus on optimization extends to feed formulation, a major cost factor in poultry production. Modern farms are employing computer-controlled systems that deftly mix feed ingredients, tailoring them to the unique nutritional needs of varying breeds at different life stages. Some farms have even incorporated real-time feed analysis, ensuring that the feed's nutritional quality remains consistently high.

Breeding, a core aspect of poultry farming, has also witnessed a technological revolution. Traditional methods are being complemented and sometimes even replaced by techniques such as artificial insemination, which allows for more controlled mating processes. The emerging practice of embryo transfer, much like its use in cattle farming, is enabling the propagation of superior genetics from donor hens to recipient hens.

Of course, disease remains a significant concern, but modern technology is proving to be an effective shield. Automated systems can now diagnose diseases by monitoring chickens' sounds or movement patterns, and vaccination robots ensure every bird in a large flock gets its due dose without undue stress.

Delving into the intricate world of genomics, poultry farmers can now make more informed breeding decisions. Marker-assisted selection, for example, allows them to identify and propagate chickens with specific genes responsible for desirable traits. The controversial realm of gene editing, with tools like CRISPR, holds the potential to bring forth birds with enhanced disease resistance or specific attributes.

Automation and robotics, meanwhile, are adding a touch of futuristic flair to poultry farms. Eggs are gently collected by robots, ensuring they remain pristine. Advanced housing systems for layers have evolved to include creature comforts like perches and nesting boxes, simulating a more natural environment for the birds.

Artificial intelligence, the darling of the tech world, is making significant inroads into poultry farming. From predictive analytics that can foresee disease outbreaks to smart algorithms that optimize resource allocation, AI is proving to be an invaluable ally.

Yet, with all these advancements, the poultry industry remains grounded in the principles of sustainability. New technologies are focusing on turning waste into wealth, with sophisticated systems transforming chicken manure into biogas or organic fertilizers. In regions grappling with water scarcity, water recycling systems stand as a testament to the industry's commitment to sustainable practices.

The modern poultry farm is a blend of tradition and technology, a place where age-old practices meet cutting-edge innovations. As the industry continues to embrace these advancements, it promises healthier birds, more efficient operations, and a sustainable future.

NETWORKING AND CONTINUED LEARNING

In the dynamic world of poultry farming, the ability to adapt, grow, and innovate is paramount. This adaptability stems not only from individual grit and determination but also from the collective wisdom of the community. And this is where the incredible value of networking and ongoing education shines through.

Engaging actively with peers, experts, and even novices in poultry farming allows for a flow of knowledge that is both invigorating and enlightening. This continuous exchange of information, from sharing successes and failures to understanding market trends, can spell the difference between merely running an operation and truly excelling in it.

Modern poultry farmers understand that they don't operate in isolation. They're part of a rich tapestry of professionals, each bringing a unique perspective and expertise. When one farmer encounters a challenge in feeding or disease management, chances are someone in their network has faced a similar hurdle. Through open communication and collaboration, solutions emerge, saving time, resources, and often, considerable heartache.

But networking isn't just about problem-solving. It's also about growth. The poultry industry, with its varying scales of operations, offers an extensive palette of experiences. From the small-scale farmer who has perfected the art of organic farming to the large-scale operator innovating with technology, there's a wealth of knowledge waiting to be tapped.

And in our digital age, networking isn't confined to the boundaries of physical proximity. Online communities, social media groups, and even webinars have expanded the horizon, connecting poultry farmers from different continents. This digital networking is a treasure trove of global insights, bringing in fresh perspectives and innovative solutions.

Yet, networking is just one side of the coin. The other, equally critical aspect is a commitment to continued learning. The world of poultry science is in constant flux, with new research findings and techniques emerging regularly. For the astute poultry farmer, staying updated is not a luxury—it's a necessity.

This thirst for knowledge can be quenched through various means. Subscriptions to scientific journals, enrollment in specialized courses, and participation in hands-on workshops are just a few avenues. The beauty of these resources is the depth and breadth they offer, catering to both beginners looking for foundational knowledge and veterans seeking advanced insights.

But as one delves into global knowledge and networks, the significance of local applicability becomes clear. Every piece of information, every new technique, needs to be viewed through the lens of local realities—be it climate, market preferences, or regulations. Striking a balance between global best practices and local nuances is the hallmark of a successful poultry operation.

In conclusion, as poultry farmers navigate the intricate dance of rearing chickens for both eggs and meat, they do so with the support of a vast community and the wisdom of continuous learning. This collaborative spirit, combined with an unyielding quest for knowledge, is what will steer the industry towards a future marked by sustainable success and innovation.

BEES: HONEY PRODUCTION AND POLLINATION

THE LIFE CYCLE OF HONEY BEES

The Beginning: From Eggs to Larvae

Honey bees, *Apis mellifera*, commence their life as tiny eggs, delicately laid by the queen bee in the hexagonal cells of the hive. A healthy queen can lay up to 1,500 eggs per day during peak season, ensuring the colony's continual growth and vitality. These eggs are about the size of a pinhead and take approximately three days to hatch.

Once hatched, the emergent larvae are immediately attended to by worker bees, or 'nurse bees,' who feed them a protein-rich secretion known as royal jelly for the first few days. Post this initial period, worker and drone larvae are transitioned to a diet consisting of honey and pollen, commonly referred to as 'bee bread.' In stark contrast, potential queen bee larvae continue to consume royal jelly throughout their developmental phase.

The Transformation: Pupation and Metamorphosis

After a feeding period that spans almost six days, the larvae are ready to move into the pupation phase. Worker bees seal off the cells containing the mature larvae with a wax capping. Inside this protective barrier, the larvae spin silk cocoons around themselves and undergo a significant transformation, metamorphosing from grub-like creatures into the more recognizable bee form. This transformative process encompasses the development of critical features, including wings, legs, and the characteristic compound eyes.

The duration of the pupation phase varies depending on the type of bee:

- Worker bees: 12-13 days

- Drones (male bees): 14-15 days

- Queens: 7-8 days

The Emergence: Birth of Adult Bees

When the metamorphosis is complete, the now fully-formed adult bee is ready to emerge. The bee will chew through the wax capping to free itself, marking its entry into the next phase of its life.

Worker bees, which form the majority of the hive's population, immediately set about performing various roles. Initially, they take on the responsibilities of nurse bees, feeding and attending to the young larvae. As they age, their duties shift to tasks like cleaning the hive, processing honey, guarding the entrance, and finally, foraging for nectar and pollen in the last stage of their life.

Drones, or male bees, have a singular primary function: to mate with a virgin queen bee. Post-mating, a drone's life ends, as the act results in its death. Those drones that do not mate face expulsion from the hive before winter, ensuring the colony's resources are reserved for the bees that contribute actively to its functioning.

The queen bee, after her brief developmental period, undertakes a series of mating flights to gather enough sperm to last her lifetime. Post these flights, her life revolves around laying eggs and secreting pheromones that maintain the colony's social order.

The Lifespan Variance

The life expectancy of a honey bee varies significantly based on its role in the colony:

- **Worker Bees:** Their lifespan ranges from 6 weeks during active seasons to 4-9 months during quieter periods. The considerable variance arises due to the strenuous nature of foraging, which can shorten their lifespan.

- **Drones:** With a life expectancy of approximately 8 weeks, drones have the shortest life cycle among honey bees. Their life either culminates in mating or in being expelled from the hive.

- **Queen Bee:** A queen bee's life is markedly longer, with many living up to 3-5 years. However, a decline in her productivity with age or health issues can lead to the colony raising a new queen to replace her.

THE STRUCTURAL ORGANIZATION OF BEE COLONIES

Hive Components: The Architectural Marvel

Every bee colony operates from its central command station: the beehive. Beyond its wooden exterior lies an intricate assembly of various components, each playing a vital role in supporting and sustaining the life inside.

Frames and Foundation: Hives are equipped with frames, rectangular structures made of wood or plastic, where bees construct their wax combs. Each frame is fitted with a foundation, usually composed of beeswax or plastic, which provides a base for bees to start their comb-building. The foundation comes embossed with hexagonal patterns mimicking the bees' natural comb structure, facilitating uniform comb construction.

Brood Chambers or Brood Boxes: This is where the queen resides and lays her eggs. Located at the hive's base, these chambers house the developing brood (eggs, larvae, and pupae). A typical hive may have one or two brood boxes, depending on the colony's size.

Super Boxes: Positioned above the brood boxes, super boxes are where bees store honey. Once filled, these frames are removed for honey extraction. Super boxes are generally shallower than brood boxes, making them lighter and easier to handle when full of honey.

Queen Excluder: A vital component, the queen excluder is a meshed screen placed between the brood boxes and the super boxes. It ensures that the queen remains in the brood chamber, preventing her from laying eggs in the honey storage area.

Hive Covers: Two types of covers usually shield a beehive:

- **Inner Cover:** Provides an insulating air space and ensures easier removal of the top cover as bees don't glue it down with propolis.
- **Outer Cover or Telescoping Cover:** The external protective shield against weather elements. It typically extends over the hive's sides, ensuring rainwater doesn't seep in.

Hive Stand: Elevating the hive off the ground, the hive stand offers protection against dampness and ground-dwelling predators.

The Hierarchy: Division of Labor

Bee colonies epitomize social organization. The colony, often numbering in tens of thousands, divides its members into three primary roles: the queen, workers, and drones.

The Queen Bee: The sole egg-laying member of the colony, the queen's primary function is reproduction. Aided by her uniquely elongated abdomen, she can lay up to 1,500 eggs daily during peak seasons. However, her responsibilities aren't just reproductive. She secretes pheromones, chemical signals that maintain social order within the colony, influencing behaviors like suppressing workers from laying eggs and maintaining cohesion among members.

Worker Bees: All female but sterile, worker bees form the colony's backbone. Their responsibilities span a spectrum of activities:

- **Nurse Bees:** Tend to the brood, feeding larvae, and maintaining optimal brood chamber conditions.
- **Builders:** Secretes beeswax to construct and repair the comb.

- ☐ **Guard Bees:** Protect the hive entrance against intruders, be it other bees or predators.
- ☐ **Foragers:** Venture out in search of nectar, pollen, water, and propolis.
- ☐ **Processors:** Convert nectar into honey by evaporating its water content and adding enzymes.
- ☐ **Undertakers:** Remove dead or diseased bees from the hive.

Drones: These male bees have a singular focus: mating with virgin queens. Lacking stingers, they don't participate in defense. Post mating, their purpose is fulfilled, and they often face expulsion from the hive, especially during resource-scarce periods.

The Communication: Waggle Dance and Pheromones

For a colony to function seamlessly, effective communication methods are paramount. Honey bees have perfected the art of communication through elaborate 'waggle dances' and pheromone secretions.

Waggle Dance: When a forager bee discovers a rich nectar or pollen source, it returns to the hive and performs a characteristic dance. The dance's direction indicates the food source's direction, the duration signifies the distance, and the vigor represents the source's richness. Through this dance, foragers efficiently communicate essential details, optimizing the colony's foraging efforts.

Pheromones: These chemical messengers play pivotal roles in maintaining hive order. The queen's pheromone, for instance, signals her presence and suppresses worker bees' egg-laying abilities. Alarm pheromones alert the colony to potential threats, while foraging pheromones mark rich food sources.

Comb Construction: Precision in Wax

Central to a hive's structural organization is the honeycomb, meticulously constructed using beeswax secreted by worker bees. These hexagonal cells are multifunctional, serving as storage for honey, pollen, and as chambers for the developing brood. The choice of a hexagon isn't random; it is the most efficient shape, using the least amount of building material to store the most amount of honey while providing the most substantial structure.

Beeswax production requires significant energy, with bees consuming approximately eight times the honey amount to produce a comb equivalent in weight. Therefore, preserving and recycling combs is a sustainable practice modern farm owners adopt, ensuring bees invest their energy more in honey production than comb building.

Symbiotic Relationships: Beneficial Hive Inhabitants

A bee colony isn't just bees. Several organisms coexist within the hive, forming mutualistic relationships with bees. Some of these beneficial inhabitants include:

- **Pseudoscorpions:** Tiny creatures that feed on hive pests like Varroa mites and wax moths.
- **Braula coeca or Bee Louse:** Harmless wingless flies that feed on bees' food but don't cause any harm.

Understanding the hive's structural organization and the intricacies of its inhabitants is crucial for every farm owner. It's not just about honey production; it's about ensuring a harmonious environment that facilitates the health and productivity of every colony member. As with any livestock or crop, knowledge empowers better management practices, and with bees, it ensures the thriving of an insect so vital to our own survival.

HONEY PRODUCTION PROCESS

The Journey from Nectar to Honey

Honey, a sweet, golden liquid that has been cherished for its taste and medicinal qualities for millennia, is a result of bees' industriousness and a sequence of sophisticated processes.

Nectar Collection: The Raw Material

Nectar, the precursor of honey, is a sugary fluid produced by flowering plants. This substance not only attracts pollinators like bees but also serves as their primary source of energy. Worker bees, specifically the foragers, are tasked with locating and retrieving nectar from flowers. Using their specially adapted mouthparts, they suck out the nectar and store it in their honey stomachs, separate from their primary digestive stomach.

Enzymatic Transformation: Adding the Bee Touch

As the bee returns to the hive, it begins to process the nectar. The bee adds enzymes, primarily invertase, from its salivary glands to the stored nectar. This enzyme starts the breakdown of the complex sugars (mainly sucrose) in the nectar into simpler forms, predominantly glucose and fructose.

Transfer and Storage: A Collaborative Effort

Once back at the hive, the forager transfers the nectar to house bees. This transfer involves regurgitating the nectar multiple times, allowing further enzymatic action and mixing. This repetitive process ensures a uniform consistency and further sugar breakdown.

After processing, house bees then store this nectar in the cells of honeycombs. At this stage, the fluid still has a high water content, rendering it unsuitable for long-term storage.

Water Reduction: Crafting the Perfect Consistency

Bees exhibit impeccable engineering skills when it comes to honey production. To reduce the water content of the stored nectar (often above 70%), bees employ a technique of fanning. They use their wings to create airflow within the hive, accelerating the evaporation process. Their objective is to bring the water content of honey down to a safe level of 18-20%, ensuring its preservation and preventing fermentation.

Capping: Sealing the Gold

Once the honey reaches its desired consistency, bees seal the honey-filled cells with beeswax. This wax cap ensures the honey remains uncontaminated and preserved. The beeswax covering is both air and water-tight, maintaining the honey's moisture level and keeping it safe from external contaminants.

Factors Influencing Honey Quality and Composition

While the fundamental process remains consistent, various factors can influence the final product's quality, taste, and composition.

Floral Source: The Foundation of Flavor and Color

The type of flowers bees predominantly forage on determines the honey's flavor, color, and aroma. For instance, clover honey is light and mild, while buckwheat honey is dark with a strong, robust flavor.

Climate and Geography: Regional Nuances

The region and its climatic conditions also play a role in honey's composition. Honey produced in humid climates might have a slightly higher water content, while those from arid regions might be denser.

Hive Health: The Importance of Vigilance

A healthy bee colony invariably produces high-quality honey. Any presence of diseases or pests, such as the Varroa mite, can compromise honey production. Regular hive inspections and timely interventions are essential.

Harvesting Time: Patience Pays

Honey's maturity determines its quality. Harvesting too early can yield honey with higher water content, making it prone to fermentation. On the other hand, allowing honey to mature and ensuring it's capped ensures a superior product.

Extraction and Processing Methods: Retaining Nature's Goodness

The manner in which honey is extracted and processed post-harvest plays a role in its quality. For instance, raw, unfiltered honey contains pollen and is often cloudier, while ultra-filtered honey is clear but might lack some natural constituents.

Advanced Techniques in Honey Production

In contemporary beekeeping, several advancements have been made to enhance honey production efficiency.

Controlled Foraging: Monofloral Honey Production

Some beekeepers practice controlled foraging, where bees are exposed only to specific flower types, resulting in monofloral honey with distinct flavors, like orange blossom or acacia honey.

Automated Extraction: The Centrifuge System

Many modern beekeepers employ centrifuge systems, where frames containing honeycombs are placed in an extractor that spins them, allowing honey to be separated by centrifugal force. This method is efficient and ensures minimal damage to the combs.

Monitoring and Analytics: Embracing Technology

Advanced hive monitoring systems, equipped with sensors and data analytics capabilities, provide real-time insights into hive health, environmental conditions, and honey production rates. Such data-driven insights can guide beekeepers in making informed decisions, optimizing both hive health and honey yield.

In essence, honey production is a delicate interplay of nature's brilliance and bee's industriousness. As modern farm owners, understanding these processes and intricacies, and complementing them with advanced methodologies, ensures that the golden elixir's production is not only optimized but also retains its natural goodness.

THE CRITICAL ROLE OF BEES IN POLLINATION

Pollination: An Overview

Pollination is a vital process in the reproductive cycle of most flowering plants. It involves the transfer of pollen grains from the male part of a flower (anther) to the female part (stigma) of the same or another flower. Successful pollination results in the production of viable seeds, ensuring the continuation of plant species. While some plants rely on wind or water for pollination, a significant number depend on animals – primarily insects, and among them, bees stand out as the champions of this process.

Why Bees?

Bees are, by evolutionary design, remarkably efficient pollinators. Several factors contribute to their preeminence:

Hairy Bodies: Unlike some other insects, bees have hairy bodies. These hairs trap pollen grains when bees visit flowers, aiding in unintentional pollen transfer as they move from bloom to bloom.

Specialized Diet: Bees rely primarily on nectar and pollen for their nutrition. This makes flowers their primary food source, ensuring frequent visits.

Fidelity to Plants: Some bee species exhibit flower constancy, meaning they preferentially visit flowers of a single species during a foraging trip. This behavior increases the probability of successful cross-pollination.

Advanced Communication: Honeybees, especially, have evolved a sophisticated communication system. The renowned "waggle dance" is a method by which bees communicate the location of rich nectar sources to their hive mates.

Impact on Agricultural Systems

The relationship between bees and agriculture is mutually beneficial. While crops provide bees with abundant food sources, bees ensure higher yields through efficient pollination.

Increased Yields: Many crops experience a significant increase in yield when adequately pollinated by bees. The exact improvement can vary based on the crop but is invariably beneficial for farm productivity.

Improved Quality: Beyond just yield, bee pollination often leads to better quality produce. For instance, fruits pollinated by bees are generally more uniform in size, juicier, and have fewer deformities.

Crop Diversity: Bees play a role in cultivating a diverse food system. Many of the foods in diverse diets, from almonds to zucchinis, owe their existence to the pollination prowess of bees.

Bee Diversity and Pollination

Not all bees are the same when it comes to pollination. The bee kingdom is vast, with over 20,000 known species, each with its unique traits and preferences.

Honeybees: The European honeybee (*Apis mellifera*) is perhaps the best-known pollinator, and for a good reason. It's a generalist, meaning it pollinates a wide range of plants. Their colony lifestyle, with large numbers, ensures a large workforce for pollination.

Bumblebees: Bumblebees are robust, fuzzy pollinators that excel in conditions where honeybees might not, like colder climates and higher altitudes. Their ability to "buzz pollinate" makes them indispensable for crops like tomatoes.

Solitary Bees: Unlike honeybees or bumblebees that live in colonies, most bee species are solitary. Mason bees and leafcutter bees are examples. They might not produce honey, but when it comes to pollination, they are often more efficient than their colonial counterparts.

Specialist Bees: Some bees have evolved alongside specific plants, becoming primary pollinators for those species. Their bodies might be adapted to access nectar from certain flower types, or they might have behavioral adaptations ensuring effective pollination of those plants.

Threats to Bee-Pollinated Systems

Despite their importance, bees face numerous threats, which, in turn, jeopardize the plants and crops they pollinate.

Pesticides: Certain chemicals, especially neonicotinoids, are known to harm bees. They can impact bee navigation, foraging behavior, and even lead to colony collapse in severe cases.

Habitat Loss: As natural landscapes give way to urban sprawl or monoculture farms, bees lose the diverse habitats they need. This not only affects their food sources but also their nesting sites, especially for solitary bees.

Diseases and Pests: Pathogens like Nosema and pests like the Varroa mite can devastate bee populations. In a globalized world, the spread of such threats becomes even more pronounced.

Climate Change: Altered weather patterns, unseasonal temperature fluctuations, and extreme weather events can disrupt the natural lifecycle of bees and the plants they rely on.

Modern Farming Practices and Bee Conservation

As a modern farm owner, recognizing the importance of bees in pollination necessitates actions that ensure their conservation.

Integrated Pest Management (IPM): Rather than relying solely on chemical pesticides, IPM focuses on a holistic approach, employing natural predators, crop rotation, and targeted treatments, reducing harm to beneficial insects like bees.

Planting for Bees: Diversifying farms by integrating bee-friendly plants or allowing native vegetation to thrive at the peripheries can offer bees the necessary forage. Plants that bloom sequentially ensure year-round food for bees.

Providing Habitats: Installing bee hotels, leaving patches of bare ground for ground-nesting bees, or having deadwood can offer nesting sites for various bee species.

Continuous Learning and Collaboration: Engaging with local beekeepers, entomologists, and conservationists can offer insights into region-specific best practices. Collaborative efforts can lead to solutions that benefit both agriculture and bee populations.

In the grand tapestry of nature, bees hold a special place as pollinators. Their unassuming yet critical role ensures the continuity of many plant species and enriches agricultural bounty. Recognizing and supporting their contributions is not just an ecological imperative but also an economic one for forward-thinking farm owners.

SETTING UP AN APIARY

Location and Environmental Considerations

Site Selection: When establishing an apiary, one of the primary considerations is location. The site should offer bees access to diverse forage sources, including a variety of flowering plants. It should also be away from areas of heavy pesticide use or pollution sources, ensuring bee health and honey purity.

Microclimate: A slight elevation or slope can help in keeping the hives dry, as water will naturally flow away. Hives should ideally be placed in locations that receive morning sunlight, as this encourages bees to start foraging earlier.

Water Source: Bees require a consistent water source, especially during warm months. A nearby stream, pond, or even a regularly filled shallow water container can serve this purpose. The water source should be within a reasonable distance, but not too close to the hives to avoid excessive moisture.

Choosing Bee Species

Different bee species have unique characteristics, making some more suitable for certain environments or purposes than others.

Apis mellifera (European honeybee): Known for their adaptability and significant honey production, they are the most popular choice for commercial beekeeping.

Apis cerana (Asian honeybee): Smaller than their European counterparts, they are adapted to tropical climates and are resistant to some pests and diseases.

Apis dorsata (Giant honeybee): These are wild bees, known for building large external combs. They aren't typically used for commercial purposes due to their aggressive nature.

Apis florea (Dwarf honeybee): These bees are also wild and aren't generally used in commercial beekeeping.

Hive Selection

Hive design can significantly impact bee health, productivity, and ease of management. There are multiple types of hives, each with its advantages:

Langstroth Hive: This is the most commonly used hive in many countries. Its design, characterized by vertically hung frames, allows for easy inspections and honey extraction without destroying the comb.

Top Bar Hive: Unlike the Langstroth, this hive design is horizontal. It's more natural for bees as they build their comb downward. It's less intrusive but might not be as efficient for honey production.

Warre Hive: Designed to mimic the vertical nature of tree hollows, this hive is less hands-on than the Langstroth, aiming to allow bees to function as naturally as possible.

Flow Hive: A more recent innovation, the Flow Hive allows for honey extraction directly from the hive without disturbing the bees or removing frames.

Installing the Bees

Once you've selected a hive, it's time to introduce the bees. There are three primary methods:

Package Bees: This is essentially a box of bees, typically sold by weight, with a separate mated queen. Once introduced to a hive, they'll establish a new colony.

Nucleus Colony (Nuc): A Nuc is a mini hive, complete with frames, brood, bees, and a mated queen. They offer a head start compared to package bees.

Swarm: Capturing a wild swarm can be a cost-effective way to populate a hive, though it does come with challenges, including uncertain bee health and temperament.

Feeding Your Bees

Newly installed bees or colonies during scarcity periods might need supplemental feeding.

Sugar Syrup: A mix of sugar and water can mimic nectar. The ratio can vary depending on the season and the specific needs of the colony.

Pollen Substitute: In areas or seasons where pollen is scarce, bees can be given a pollen substitute to ensure they get the required proteins.

Regular Hive Inspection

Regular inspections are crucial to ascertain the health and productivity of the hive. While being as non-intrusive as possible:

Monitor Brood Patterns: Consistent brood patterns indicate a healthy queen. Spotty patterns might suggest issues like disease or an aging queen.

Check for Pests and Diseases: Regularly inspect for signs of common threats like Varroa mites, Nosema, or American Foulbrood.

Evaluate Food Stores: Ensure bees have enough honey and pollen, especially approaching winter or during droughts.

Queen Presence: Ensure that a productive queen is present. If not, the colony might need requeening.

Pest and Disease Management

An apiary is susceptible to various pests and diseases. Adopting a proactive approach can prevent many of these issues:

Varroa Mites: These are among the most significant threats to bee colonies globally. Regular monitoring and treatments, like oxalic acid vaporization or formic acid strips, can manage mite levels.

American Foulbrood: This bacterial disease can decimate colonies. Infected hives should be quarantined and equipment sterilized.

Wax Moths: Their larvae can destroy combs. Good apiary hygiene and regular inspections can prevent significant damage.

Small Hive Beetles: They feed on pollen, honey, and brood. Keeping hives strong and healthy can deter these pests.

Harvesting Honey

The reward of beekeeping is, of course, the honey. However, it's essential to strike a balance to ensure that bees have enough stores for themselves, especially during winter.

Frame Inspection: Only frames that are at least 80% capped with wax should be harvested.

Extraction Process: Depending on the hive type, honey can be extracted using centrifugal force in a honey extractor or directly from Flow Hives.

Filtration and Bottling: Once extracted, honey is typically filtered to remove any debris before bottling.

Scaling and Commercial Considerations

For those considering commercial beekeeping:

Equipment Upgrades: Consider investing in equipment that can handle larger quantities, like larger extractors or automated frame handlers.

Diversified Products: Beyond honey, consider products like beeswax, propolis, or even bee pollen.

Regulatory Compliance: Ensure understanding and compliance with local regulations, including labeling requirements, quality standards, and health regulations.

Market Research: Understand the target market. Organic, raw, or single-source honeys might fetch higher prices in certain markets.

In the realm of beekeeping, continuous learning is vital. Nature, with its dynamic challenges and rewards, ensures that the beekeeper's journey is ever-evolving. Embracing best practices, staying updated with research, and networking with fellow beekeepers can ensure a thriving, productive apiary that benefits both the bees and the keeper.

BEST PRACTICES IN BEE MANAGEMENT

Sustainable Beekeeping Practices

Bee-Centric Approach: While honey and other bee by-products are essential, it's crucial to prioritize bee welfare. For instance, always leave enough honey for the colony's nutritional needs, especially during non-foraging seasons, rather than prioritizing maximum extraction.

Diverse Foraging Opportunities: Ensure your bees have access to a diverse range of flowering plants. Monocultures, often resulting from industrial farming practices, limit the bees' diet, affecting their health and the quality of the honey they produce.

Regular Monitoring and Inspection

Routine hive inspections can preempt many issues, from diseases to potential swarming. While inspecting:

Assess Colony Strength: Regularly check the population size, brood pattern, and behavior of worker bees. A dwindling population or erratic worker behavior could indicate a problem.

Evaluate Queen's Performance: A robust and healthy queen is vital for colony success. Monitor the queen's egg-laying pattern and replace an underperforming queen.

Monitor Food Stores: Even if bees have access to forage, there might be periods when nectar flow is minimal. Regularly assess honey and pollen stores and provide supplemental feeding when necessary.

Managing Bee Health

Integrated Pest Management (IPM): Adopt an IPM approach, which prioritizes non-chemical control methods and only uses chemicals as a last resort. For example, physical barriers, like drone comb trapping, can be used to manage Varroa mites.

Disease Identification and Treatment: Quick identification and timely treatment of diseases can save a colony. Whether it's the bacterial threat of American Foulbrood or the fungal challenge from Nosema, knowing the signs and acting promptly is critical.

Swarm Management

Swarming is a natural bee behavior, indicating a healthy colony. However, from a beekeeping perspective, it can result in a significant loss of worker bees, affecting honey production.

Regular Inspections: During swarming season, increase the frequency of hive inspections. Identifying and removing swarm cells can prevent the swarm.

Provide Space: A common reason bees swarm is due to space constraints. Regularly adding brood boxes or supers when the existing ones are near capacity can prevent swarming.

Requeening: Older queens are more likely to lead a swarm. Regularly replacing the queen, typically every 1-2 years, can minimize swarming tendencies.

Hive Placement and Environmental Management

Shelter from Extremes: Hives should be placed in locations that protect bees from extreme weather conditions, be it scorching sun or chilling winds.

Adequate Ventilation: Bees require oxygen, and good airflow helps in regulating the hive's internal temperature. Ensure hives have adequate ventilation, especially during hot months.

Water Access: Bees need water for various purposes, including cooling the hive. Ensure there's a water source nearby, but remember that stagnant water can become a breeding ground for mosquitoes.

Wintering Bees

In regions with cold winters, bees need special care:

Food Stores: Bees consume more honey during winter. Check stores in late autumn and supplement with sugar syrup if needed.

Hive Insulation: Protecting the hive from chilling winds and snow can be achieved by adding insulation. However, ensure the hive still has proper ventilation.

Reduce Hive Entrances: A smaller entrance prevents drafts and also makes it easier for bees to defend against pests.

Sustainable Harvesting Practices

Ethical Harvesting: Only harvest from colonies that have excess honey. Remember, bees work hard for their stores, and they require it for sustenance.

Frame Selection: Only remove frames that are at least 80% capped. The capped honey has the right moisture content and will store well.

Gentle Handling: When extracting honey, handle frames gently to minimize damage. Bees invest significant effort into building comb, and preserving it can save them labor.

Education and Continuous Learning

Beekeeping practices and challenges evolve. Staying informed is crucial:

Attend Workshops: Regularly attend beekeeping workshops. They provide insights into new methodologies, tools, and can be a platform to discuss challenges with peers.

Join Beekeeping Associations: Local or national beekeeping associations can be treasure troves of information and support.

Stay Updated with Research: With the global concern for bee populations, there's continuous research on bee health, behavior, and management. Being informed of the latest findings can greatly benefit bee management practices.

Engage with the Broader Community

Promote Bee-Friendly Practices: Engage with local farmers and gardeners to promote the planting of bee-friendly flowers and reduce pesticide usage.

Beekeeping Workshops: Offer workshops or open days where the community can learn about bees, their importance, and how they can support local bee populations.

Collaborate: Collaborate with local schools, universities, and research institutions. It promotes understanding, fosters a sense of community, and can lead to valuable partnerships.

Mastering the art of beekeeping is a continuous journey, influenced by the ever-changing dynamics of nature. However, with commitment, continuous learning, and best practices, it's possible to ensure both the health of the bees and the success of the apiary.

BEE HEALTH AND COMMON CHALLENGES

Understanding Bee Physiology

To maintain the health of a bee colony, one must first grasp the nuances of bee physiology:

Digestive System: Bees' primary nutrition sources are nectar, which provides carbohydrates, and pollen, which gives proteins, lipids, vitamins, and minerals. Their digestive system, comprising the crop (or honey stomach), midgut, and hindgut, is designed to extract nutrients from these foods.

Respiratory System: Unlike mammals, bees respire through a tracheal system, which involves a series of tubes and spiracles. This system allows for direct oxygen flow to tissues and carbon dioxide release.

Circulatory System: Bees possess an open circulatory system. Hemolymph, akin to blood in vertebrates, circulates nutrients, waste, and hormones throughout the body.

Pest and Parasite Challenges

Varroa Destructor Mites: These are the most notorious threats to honey bee colonies. These parasitic mites attach to bees, weakening them by sucking hemolymph and transmitting viruses.
Management: Integrated pest management strategies include drone brood removal, where mites are typically most concentrated, and organic treatments like formic or oxalic acid during periods when brood is minimal.

Tracheal Mites: These micro-sized mites infiltrate the bees' tracheal system, impeding their ability to breathe.
Management: Resistant bee strains and menthol treatments can be effective deterrents against tracheal mites.

Nosema: A microsporidian that affects the bees' midgut. Infected bees have reduced lifespans and can exhibit unusual behavior like premature foraging.
Management: Regular hive inspections, ensuring good hive ventilation, and replacing old combs can help in preventing nosema infestations.

Diseases Impacting Bee Health

American Foulbrood (AFB): Caused by the bacterium *Paenibacillus larvae*, AFB is lethal to bee larvae. It's marked by a foul odor and capped brood appearing sunken or perforated.
Management: Unfortunately, once a colony is infected, it usually must be destroyed to prevent spread. To prevent AFB, regularly inspect hives and practice good apiary hygiene.

European Foulbrood (EFB): Unlike AFB, EFB affects bee larvae before the capped stage. Caused by the bacterium *Melissococcus plutonius*, it leads to yellow, twisted larvae that eventually turn brown and die.
Management: Hive hygiene, requeening, and in extreme cases, antibiotic treatments can help manage EFB.

Chalkbrood: A fungal disease where affected larvae harden and appear chalk-like.
Management: Improving hive ventilation and occasionally requeening can assist in mitigating chalkbrood.

Sacbrood: A viral illness leading to larvae death post capping. Affected larvae turn pale and fluid-filled.
Management: Requeening is the primary method of addressing sacbrood.

Environmental Stressors

Pesticides: Neonicotinoids and other chemical pesticides can be deadly to bees or impact their foraging behavior and reproductive abilities.
Management: Collaborate with local farmers to employ bee-friendly farming methods and minimize pesticide usage during foraging hours.

Habitat Loss: Urbanization and monoculture farming reduce the diversity of flora available to bees.
Management: Encourage the planting of bee-friendly flora in gardens, parks, and public spaces. Beekeepers can also diversify their apiary surroundings.

Climate Change: Altered weather patterns can disrupt the blooming patterns of plants bees rely on.
Management: Beekeepers might need to relocate their apiaries to areas with more consistent and reliable foraging options.

Bee Nutrition and Starvation

Importance of Nutrition: A balanced diet is crucial for bee health, immunity, and productivity. Pollen provides proteins and lipids, while nectar gives them carbohydrates.
Signs of Malnutrition: A colony deprived of balanced nutrition can exhibit reduced brood rearing, diminished honey stores, increased susceptibility to diseases, and a weaker overall colony demeanor.
Management: Regularly inspect hives to ensure they have adequate food stores. During shortages, provide supplemental feeding in the form of sugar syrups or pollen substitutes.

Winter Starvation: In colder regions, bees rely heavily on stored honey during winter. Inadequate stores can lead to starvation.
Management: Monitor honey stores in late autumn and provide supplemental feeding to ensure colonies have enough food to last the winter.

Managing Aggressive Bees

Causes of Aggression: Factors such as genetics, environmental stressors, or disturbances can make a bee colony more aggressive.
Management: Requeening with a gentler bee strain, reducing disturbances near the apiary, and using smoke during inspections can reduce aggression.

Genetic Management for Healthier Colonies

Breeding for Resistance: By selecting bees with natural resistance to diseases and pests, beekeepers can breed stronger and more resilient colonies.

Avoiding Inbreeding: Regularly introducing new genetic material, either by purchasing queens from reputable breeders or practicing controlled mating, can prevent inbreeding and its associated health complications.

The health and vitality of bee colonies are an amalgamation of various factors, from their immediate environment to broader ecological shifts. As modern farm owners, understanding, anticipating, and preemptively addressing these challenges ensures not just the well-being of the bees but also the prosperity of the entire farming ecosystem. With an informed approach to bee health, one can foster resilient and productive colonies, ensuring a steady yield of honey and the myriad benefits of pollination.

REARING RABBITS

Selection of Breeds

Rabbits are versatile creatures, with different breeds offering unique characteristics. Here are the primary factors to consider when selecting rabbit breeds:

Purpose of Rearing: Are you rearing them for meat, fur, wool, show, or as pets?

Climate Tolerance: Some breeds are better adapted to cold climates, while others thrive in warmer regions.

Growth Rate & Size: For meat production, breeds that grow rapidly and attain a significant size are preferable.

Temperament: If breeding for pets or show, a gentle temperament is essential.

Popular breeds include:

New Zealand Whites: Favored for meat due to their size and growth rate.

Rex: Known for their plush fur.

Angora: Prized for their long wool, which can be spun.

Mini Lop: Popular as pets for their small size and friendly nature.

Housing and Environment

Rabbit housing must prioritize safety, comfort, and hygiene.

Hutches: A raised wooden enclosure, offering protection from predators and damp ground. Ensure it has a waterproof roof and wire mesh for ventilation.

Pens: An enclosed area allowing rabbits to roam, graze, and exercise. Must be secure to prevent escape and intrusion by predators.

Flooring: Solid flooring can be used with bedding, such as straw or hay, to absorb waste and provide comfort. Alternatively, wire mesh floors facilitate waste drop-through but should be of a size that avoids foot injury.

Environmental Control: In regions with extreme temperatures, consider temperature control mechanisms. Ensure adequate shade, ventilation, and protection from drafts.

Nutrition and Feeding

A rabbit's diet is foundational to its health, growth, and productivity.

Hay: The primary diet. Timothy hay, meadow hay, and other grass hays are excellent sources of fiber, aiding digestion and dental health.

Pellets: Commercially available, they're fortified with essential vitamins and minerals. Ensure they're fresh and of high quality.

Greens: Fresh vegetables like broccoli, carrots, and lettuce can be offered. Introduce gradually to avoid digestive issues.

Water: Fresh water must be available at all times. Use a drip-feed water bottle to keep it clean.

Breeding Practices

Age of Breeding: Female rabbits (does) can begin breeding from 5-8 months, depending on the breed, while males (bucks) are ready by 6-9 months.

Mating: Introduce the doe to the buck's cage. Monitor for aggressive behavior. Successful mating is usually indicated by the buck's characteristic fall-off.

Gestation and Kindling: The gestation period averages 30 days. Provide a nesting box filled with hay or straw for the doe 5-7 days before expected delivery.

Post-Birth: Check the litter for any deceased kits. Does will nurse their young typically once or twice daily.

Health Management

Vaccinations: Rabbits require vaccinations against diseases like Myxomatosis and Rabbit Hemorrhagic Disease. Consult a vet for a vaccination schedule.

Parasite Control: Regularly inspect for signs of internal (worms) and external (mites, fleas) parasites. Employ treatments as required.

Grooming: Some breeds, especially woolly ones, need regular grooming to prevent matting and detect skin issues.

Dental Health: Overgrown teeth can be a concern. Ensure a diet high in hay to naturally grind down their teeth.

Hygiene and Cleaning

Hutch Cleaning: Remove soiled bedding daily. Once a week, conduct a thorough cleaning, disinfecting the hutch to prevent bacterial growth.

Waste Management: Employ a regular waste removal system, especially if using solid flooring. Rabbit manure is an excellent compost material.

Record Keeping

Documenting key aspects of rabbit rearing helps in managing productivity and health.

Breeding Records: Track mating dates, gestation, birth details, and weaning dates.

Growth Charts: Monitor weight and growth rates, especially if rearing for meat.

Health Logs: Record vaccinations, treatments, and any health incidents.

Expense and Revenue Tracking: For commercial enterprises, diligently document expenses and revenues to analyze profitability.

Rearing rabbits, whether for commercial purposes or as pets, requires a comprehensive understanding of their needs. From housing to nutrition, each aspect plays a pivotal role in ensuring their health and productivity. Modern farm owners, armed with the right knowledge and tools, can make rabbit rearing a rewarding venture, both economically and in terms of the joy these creatures bring.

REARING GUINEA PIGS

Breed Selection and Characteristics

Guinea pigs, also known as cavies, come in various breeds, each with its unique set of features:

American: Short, smooth, and glossy coat; a popular breed for beginners.

Abyssinian: Distinguished by rosettes or swirls in their fur, giving them a somewhat rumpled appearance.

Peruvian: Renowned for its long, silky hair which can grow several inches in length.

Silkie (or Sheltie): Smooth long hair that flows back from the face without the presence of a noticeable parting.

Rex: Short, dense, and plush fur with a gentle curl, accompanied by a curly whisker.

When choosing a breed, consider the purpose (pet, show, or breeding), the required maintenance, and individual aesthetics preferences.

Housing Requirements

Cage Size: A minimum of 7.5 square feet for one guinea pig, but they prefer companionship, so a larger cage for pairs or groups is recommended.

Flooring: A solid base is essential. Wire-bottom cages can harm their delicate feet.

Bedding: Use absorbent materials like paper or aspen shavings. Cedar or pine shavings, although popular, might contain harmful oils.

Enrichment: Include hideaways, tunnels, and toys for stimulation.

Location: The cage should be placed in a quiet, draft-free location with moderate temperatures.

Dietary Needs

Hay: Fresh hay should be available at all times. Timothy hay is particularly suitable, as it's an excellent source of fiber and aids in digestive health.

Pellets: Commercial guinea pig pellets supplement their diet with necessary nutrients.

Fresh Veggies: Green leafy vegetables can be introduced. Foods like broccoli, zucchini, and bell peppers are suitable.

Vitamin C: Guinea pigs cannot produce Vitamin C and need external sources. Ensure their diet includes Vitamin C-rich foods or supplements.

Water: A constant supply of fresh water, ideally in a drip-feed bottle, is crucial.

Breeding and Lifecycle

Sexual Maturity: Females (sows) reach maturity at 2 months, while males (boars) can be a little earlier.

Gestation Period: Typically lasts 59-72 days, a notably long duration compared to other rodents.

Litter Size: Averages 2-4 pups but can range from 1-6.

Post-Birth: Pups are born fully furred, eyes open, and can eat solid food within a day. However, they'll continue to nurse for the first few weeks.

Handling and Social Needs

Regular Interaction: Guinea pigs are social animals. Frequent, gentle handling enhances their tame nature.

Companionship: They thrive in pairs or groups. However, ensure same-sex groupings or ensure neutering to prevent unintended breeding.

Healthcare

Regular Checkups: Routine vet visits help in early detection of potential health issues.

Grooming: Depending on the breed, regular grooming can prevent matted fur and detect skin problems.

Signs of Illness: Lethargy, difficulty in breathing, refusal to eat, or crusty eyes are signs that warrant immediate attention.

Dental Health: Their teeth grow continuously. Chew toys and a proper diet help wear them down.

Hygiene and Maintenance

Cage Cleaning: Frequent cleaning, at least once a week, prevents ammonia build-up from their urine. Spot cleaning daily is advisable.

Bathing: Only bathe when necessary, as guinea pigs can find it stressful. When done, use lukewarm water and guinea pig-specific shampoo.

Nail Trimming: Their nails grow continually and may require monthly trimming. A regular clipper can work, but be cautious of the quick.

Record-Keeping for Profitability

If rearing guinea pigs for economic benefits, maintaining comprehensive records is paramount:

Breeding Records: Monitor mating, birth dates, and litter sizes.

Growth Records: Regular weight checks can highlight potential health issues.

Expense Tracking: Log food, bedding, and medical costs.

Sales Records: Track sales of guinea pigs, noting dates, prices, and buyer details.

Rearing guinea pigs, with their relatively easy management and minimal space requirements, can be a rewarding venture for modern farm owners. With the right techniques, these small animals can provide both emotional and financial returns. Whether one's focus is on breeding, exhibition, or merely companionship, understanding the intricacies of guinea pig care is essential.

REARING GOATS

Breed Selection and Characteristics

Selecting the right breed is pivotal in determining the purpose of rearing goats - be it for milk, meat, fiber, or as show animals.

Dairy Breeds: Nubian, LaMancha, Alpine, and Saanen are recognized for their milk-producing capacity.

Meat Breeds: Boer, Kiko, and Spanish goats are particularly reared for meat.

Fiber Breeds: Angora goats produce mohair, while Cashmere goats yield cashmere wool.

Dwarf Breeds: Nigerian Dwarf and Pygmy goats are small-sized, ideal for homesteads with space constraints or for show purposes.

Housing Requirements

Shelter: While goats are hearty animals, they require protection from extreme weather conditions. Barns or three-sided shelters are effective.

Fencing: Strong fencing, like cattle panels or chain-link fences, is essential to keep goats contained and safe from predators.

Bedding: Dry straw or wood shavings work best. Regularly cleaning and replacing bedding is critical for sanitation.

Climbing and Playing Structures: Goats are curious and active; providing them with platforms or ramps can be beneficial for their well-being.

Nutritional Needs

Forage: Fresh pasture or good-quality hay should be the primary food source. Alfalfa, clover, and perennial peanut hay are suitable choices.

Grains: Depending on the purpose (meat, milk, or breeding), supplemental grain feed might be necessary.

Minerals: Free-choice mineral supplements, specifically designed for goats, should be accessible at all times.

Clean Water: A constant supply of fresh water is crucial, especially for lactating does.

Breeding Practices

Mating Season: Many goat breeds are seasonal breeders, with fall being the typical mating time.

Age of Breeding: Does can start breeding at around 7-8 months, but it's advisable to wait until they are physically mature at about 18-24 months.

Gestation Period: Roughly 150 days (5 months).

Birthing: Also known as 'kidding', it's essential to monitor does for signs of labor and ensure a clean, quiet place for birthing.

Disease Prevention and Health Care

Routine Checkups: Regular health evaluations, including fecal tests for internal parasites, are paramount.

Vaccination: Essential vaccines include those against clostridial diseases (CDT) and tetanus.

Hoof Care: Hooves must be inspected and trimmed every 4-8 weeks to prevent overgrowth and associated complications.

Parasite Management: Both internal and external parasites can be detrimental. Regular deworming and external parasite control measures should be in place.

Milking Practices (For Dairy Goats)

Milking Schedule: Most dairy goats are milked twice daily, usually 12 hours apart.

Milking Hygiene: Ensuring clean udders, hands, and equipment is vital to prevent bacterial contamination.

Mastitis Control: Regularly checking for signs of mastitis, an inflammation of the mammary gland, ensures timely treatment and continued milk quality.

Record Keeping

Comprehensive documentation is indispensable for optimizing profitability and maintaining herd health:

Breeding Records: Details about sires, breeding dates, and expected kidding dates.

Milk Production Records: Daily milk yield for dairy goats.

Health Records: Document vaccinations, deworming, illnesses, and treatments.

Growth and Weight Records: Useful for monitoring the health and development of kids.

Sales and Expense Records: Keeping tabs on revenues and expenses assists in determining profitability.

Market Dynamics

Understanding the market demand, whether it's for goat meat (chevon), milk, or fiber, helps in making informed decisions about herd size, breeding practices, and potential sales avenues. Research on local consumer preferences, export opportunities, and niche markets (organic, free-range, etc.) is invaluable.

Sustainability Practices

Incorporating sustainable practices is beneficial for the environment, the goats, and the farm's economic viability:

Rotational Grazing: This method enhances pasture longevity, reduces parasite load, and ensures a steady food supply.

Natural Pest Control: Using methods like beneficial insects, or birds can reduce the reliance on chemical treatments.

Rainwater Harvesting: Implementing systems to collect and store rainwater can decrease water expenses.

Rearing goats requires a blend of dedication, knowledge, and patience. With their multifaceted utility, from providing nourishing milk to high-quality meat, these resilient animals are a valuable addition to any modern farm. Ensuring their well-being through proper care, nutrition, and health practices will, in turn, ensure a farm's productivity and profitability.

REARING QUAIL

Species and Breed Consideration

Quails come in a variety of species, each with its own unique characteristics. Some of the most prominent are:

Coturnix Quail: Also known as the Japanese quail, these birds mature quickly, are excellent layers, and are typically raised for both meat and eggs.

Bobwhite Quail: Native to North America, these are often raised for meat and hunting purposes.

Button Quail: Smallest of the quails, they're primarily ornamental and are often kept as pets or for avian exhibits.

Housing Quails

Brooder Box: Quail chicks, or 'quailings', need to be housed in a brooder box for the initial weeks. The box should be equipped with heat lamps to maintain a consistent temperature.

Cages vs. Aviaries: Adult quails can be housed in either cages or larger aviaries. Cages facilitate easier collection of eggs and make it simpler to monitor individual birds. Aviaries allow for a more natural setting but might pose challenges in terms of management.

Flooring: Wire mesh is commonly used, allowing droppings to fall through. However, solid flooring with bedding like wood shavings can also be suitable.

Space Requirements: Typically, one square foot per bird is sufficient, though giving them more space can reduce stress.

Dietary Needs

Starter Feed: Quail chicks should be fed a high-protein starter feed for the initial weeks to support rapid growth.

Layer Feed: As they mature, especially for those rearing quails for eggs, transitioning to a layer feed ensures they get the necessary nutrients.

Water: Fresh water should be consistently available. Special quail waterers, which are shallower than regular poultry waterers, prevent the birds from drowning.

Breeding Quails

Mating Ratio: A common ratio is one male to three females to ensure effective fertilization without causing undue stress to the females.

Egg Collection: Quails lay almost daily. Regular collection ensures fresh eggs and reduces the chances of the eggs getting dirty or damaged.

Incubation: Quail eggs typically take 16-18 days to hatch. Maintaining the right temperature (around 37.5°C or 99.5°F) and humidity (45% for the first 14 days, 60-65% afterward) is vital.

Health and Disease Management

Common Diseases: Like all poultry, quails can suffer from diseases like coccidiosis, avian influenza, and quail bronchitis. Awareness of symptoms and timely intervention is key.

Parasite Control: Internal parasites, as well as external ones like mites and lice, can be a concern. Regular health checks and appropriate treatments are necessary.

Vaccinations: Depending on regional prevalence, vaccinations against certain diseases might be recommended.

Harvesting and Processing

Egg Collection: For those focusing on egg production, creating a routine collection schedule ensures consistency in egg quality.

Meat Production: Coturnix quails, for instance, can be ready for processing as early as 8-10 weeks. They yield tender meat, which is considered a delicacy in many cuisines.

Record Keeping

Maintaining detailed records is invaluable for any modern farm. This should include:

Breeding Records: Track mating pairs, egg laying frequency, and hatch rates.

Health and Medication Logs: Document any signs of disease, treatments administered, and their outcomes.

Feed Consumption: Monitoring how much feed is consumed can offer insights into flock health and help forecast future feed needs.

Economic Aspects

Market Research: Understanding the demand for quail meat and eggs in the local market, as well as potential export opportunities, helps in making informed decisions.

Value Addition: Beyond selling fresh eggs and meat, there's scope for adding value. Quail eggs can be pickled, or the meat can be sold as processed gourmet products.

Diversification: While quails can be a primary focus, integrating them with other farm activities, such as vegetable farming (where they can aid in pest control), can enhance overall farm profitability.

Environmental and Sustainable Practices

Waste Management: Quail droppings can be composted and used as a high-quality fertilizer.

Free-Range vs. Caged: While caging is common, there's a growing demand for free-range quail products. Such a system aligns more closely with natural behavior, potentially resulting in better quality meat and eggs.

Integrated Farming: Quails can be raised in tandem with other animals or agricultural endeavors, making efficient use of space and resources.

Quail farming, with its quick turnover and potential for high returns, can be a rewarding venture for modern farm owners. Like all farming activities, success in rearing quails hinges on knowledge, diligent management, and a commitment to the welfare of the birds. By focusing on best practices, leveraging modern technologies, and staying informed about market trends, farm owners can carve out a profitable niche in this segment of poultry farming.

REARING DUCKS

Selection of Duck Breeds

Different breeds of ducks are suitable for various purposes such as meat, eggs, ornamental, and even pest control. Some popular breeds include:

Pekin: Widely recognized for meat production due to their rapid growth and ample size.

Khaki Campbell: Esteemed for their prolific egg-laying capabilities.

Mallard: Often kept for ornamental purposes or for hunting preserves.

Muscovy: Unique in appearance and behavior, they're known for their meat quality.

Housing Requirements

Shelter: Ducks require protection from predators and severe weather. A simple shed or duck house, with a secure door, is essential.

Flooring: While straw bedding is popular, alternatives like wood shavings can also be used. Wet bedding should be replaced promptly to prevent fungal infections.

Ponds and Water Access: While not strictly necessary, ducks thrive when they have access to a pond or kiddie pool. This allows for natural behaviors such as foraging, swimming, and cleaning.

Space Requirements: Typically, 2-3 square feet per duck inside the house and about 15 square feet in an outdoor run is beneficial.

Feeding and Nutrition

Starter Feed: Ducklings require high-protein feed to kickstart their growth. Waterfowl starter feeds are available in the market.

Grower and Layer Feed: As ducks mature, transitioning to grower and layer feeds ensures they receive the right nutrients at different life stages.

Supplements: While commercial feeds are comprehensive, occasional supplementation with greens, worms, and small fish can benefit the ducks.

Breeding Ducks

Mating Ratio: A typical ratio is one drake (male duck) for every 2-6 ducks (females).

Nesting: Ducks need a quiet, dark, and safe place to lay their eggs. Providing straw-filled nesting boxes can encourage egg-laying.

Incubation: Duck eggs can be incubated naturally by the mother duck or using an artificial incubator, usually taking 28-30 days to hatch.

Health and Disease Management

Common Ailments: Ducks are prone to diseases like duck plague, avian influenza, and botulism. Quick detection and timely veterinary intervention can mitigate risks.

Vaccination: Depending on regional risks, vaccinations against certain diseases may be warranted.

Parasite Control: Ducks can be affected by internal and external parasites. Regular deworming and pest management are crucial.

Handling and Human Interaction

Taming Ducks: Regular interaction from a young age can make ducks more amenable to human presence.

Handling: Ducks should be held with care, supporting their full body and avoiding any undue stress.

Economic Aspects

Market Trends: Understanding the demand for duck meat, eggs, and even ornamental ducks in local and global markets can guide production.

Value Addition: Duck eggs can be sold fresh, or they can be used in specialty foods like salted eggs or balut. Similarly, duck meat can be sold fresh, smoked, or processed into sausages and other products.

Diversification: Ducks can be integrated with other farm activities. For instance, their affinity for water can be used in integrated rice-duck farming, where ducks help manage pests in paddy fields.

Environmental and Sustainable Practices

Waste Management: Duck droppings are an excellent source of nutrients for plants. Properly managed, they can be used to enrich soils or even in aquaponic systems.

Free-Range Farming: Allowing ducks to forage and roam in a controlled environment can result in healthier birds and tastier meat.

Integrated Farming Systems: Ducks can be incorporated into broader farm ecosystems, contributing to pest control, soil enrichment, and even water purification in certain setups.

Special Considerations

Molting: Ducks undergo molting, where they shed old feathers. During this period, egg production might dip, and ducks might appear scruffier.

Predator Control: Ducks can be vulnerable to predators like foxes, raccoons, and birds of prey. Proper housing, fencing, and even guardian animals can mitigate these threats.

Rearing ducks is an endeavor that can be both economically rewarding and personally fulfilling. These waterfowl, with their distinct personalities and characteristics, can be an excellent addition to diverse farming systems. Ensuring their well-being through proper management practices, while also optimizing for productivity, allows modern farm owners to realize the full potential of duck farming.

BOOK 4

CHAPTER 7

ENERGY SELF-SUFFICIENCY

INTRODUCTION TO RENEWABLE ENERGY: SOLAR, WIND, AND BIOMASS

SOLAR ENERGY: HARNESSING THE SUN'S POWER ON THE FARM

Photovoltaic (PV) Systems: Photovoltaic systems are the most commonly recognized method of capturing solar energy. They directly convert sunlight into electricity using solar cells.

Components: PV systems typically include solar panels, inverters, mounting systems, and trackers.

Placement: For optimal energy collection, these panels should be oriented toward the sun, usually at angles that capture sunlight most efficiently based on latitude and seasonal variations.

Maintenance: While PV systems have minimal moving parts, regular cleaning and occasional component checks ensure longevity.

Solar Thermal Systems: Solar thermal energy captures the sun's heat.

Applications: These systems can heat water for personal use, space heating, or even for heating in greenhouses.

Components: Solar thermal systems include solar collectors, circulation pumps, storage tanks, and heat exchangers.

Efficiency: Although solar thermal systems are generally more efficient than PV systems in converting sunlight to usable energy, their applications are more limited.

WIND ENERGY: UTILIZING AIR CURRENTS FOR POWER

Wind Turbines: These are the primary tools used to convert wind energy into electricity.

Types: Turbines can be classified mainly as horizontal-axis (most common) and vertical-axis.

Placement: Ideally, wind turbines should be situated where wind speeds are at their highest. Hilltops or open plains are usually preferable.

Maintenance: As with all mechanical systems, turbines require periodic maintenance. Bearings, gearboxes, and blades need regular checks.

Wind Assessment: Before investing in wind energy systems, it's vital to understand the wind resource of your property.

Anemometers: Devices used to measure wind speed. They can be mounted on towers to gather data over a year to gauge the feasibility of wind energy installation.

Energy Storage for Wind Power: Unlike solar, wind doesn't always follow predictable patterns. Hence, integrating battery storage can help in ensuring a steady power supply.

BIOMASS: ORGANIC MATTER AS A POWER SOURCE

Principles of Biomass Energy: Biomass energy is derived from organic material. When this organic material is burned or biologically processed, it releases the energy stored within.

Sources of Biomass: Several sources can be used, some of which may already be present on a farm.

Wood: The most commonly used biomass source, either from direct forest cuttings or wood waste.

Agricultural Residues: Leftovers from crops, such as corn stalks or wheat straw.

Animal Manure: Especially from large livestock operations, it can be a significant source of biomass energy.

Energy Crops: Some crops, like switchgrass, are grown specifically for energy production.

Conversion of Biomass into Energy: Different processes can turn biomass into usable energy.

Combustion: Directly burning biomass to produce heat, which can then be used to generate electricity.

Anaerobic Digestion: In the absence of oxygen, bacteria break down biomass to produce methane, which can be harnessed as a fuel.

Fermentation: Biomass, especially energy crops, can be fermented to produce ethanol, a biofuel.

Gasification: Under specific conditions, biomass can be converted into gas, which can then be burned for energy.

INTEGRATING RENEWABLE ENERGY SYSTEMS IN FARM OPERATIONS

Hybrid Systems: For consistent energy supply and to circumnavigate the inherent limitations of each energy source, farms can integrate multiple renewable energy systems.

Solar-Wind Hybrid: Combines the strengths of solar and wind energy. When it's not sunny, it might be windy, ensuring a more consistent energy output.

Biomass-Solar: During overcast days when solar output might be low, biomass can provide a reliable energy source.

Grid Connections and Off-grid Systems: Depending on the farm's location and energy needs, there's an option to connect renewable systems to the grid or operate entirely off-grid.

Grid-tied Systems: These allow farms to sell excess energy back to the grid, often providing a revenue source. It also ensures power availability during periods of low renewable output.

Off-grid Systems: Essential for remote farms. Such setups often rely heavily on energy storage solutions like batteries.

Energy Storage: Renewable energy, especially solar and wind, can be inconsistent. Energy storage systems, typically batteries, are crucial for ensuring a constant energy supply.

Battery Systems: Modern battery systems, like lithium-ion, provide efficient energy storage solutions. They store excess energy produced during peak renewable output periods for use during lulls.

FINANCIAL AND ENVIRONMENTAL CONSIDERATIONS

Return on Investment (ROI): While the upfront cost of renewable energy systems can be substantial, the long-term savings, coupled with potential revenue from selling excess energy, often leads to favorable ROI.

Incentives and Grants: Many governments and institutions offer financial incentives, tax breaks, or grants for farms transitioning to renewable energy sources. It's worth researching local opportunities.

Environmental Impact: Transitioning to renewables significantly reduces a farm's carbon footprint. It also positions the farm as environmentally conscious, a trait increasingly in demand among modern consumers.

Modern farming is as much about innovative practices above the ground as it is about the soil and crops. Embracing renewable energy is a testament to a farm's commitment to sustainable practices, not just in agriculture but in every aspect of its operations. As energy costs continue to rise and the global emphasis on sustainability grows, renewable energy isn't just an option; it's a necessity. The sun, wind, and organic matter offer untapped potential, waiting to be harnessed, ensuring that our farms remain productive, sustainable, and self-sufficient for generations to come.

ENERGY CONSERVATION AND ENERGY-SAVING TECHNIQUES

THE ESSENCE OF ENERGY CONSERVATION ON THE FARM

While the spotlight often shines on energy production, the mantra for a truly sustainable operation also emphasizes energy conservation. Before even discussing new technologies or practices, the modern farm owner should first look inward at their current energy consumption patterns. Often, the most significant savings come not from the installation of new technology but from the refinement of existing systems.

ASSESSMENT: YOUR FARM'S ENERGY PROFILE

Energy Audits:

Professional Audits: Hiring professionals to assess your farm's energy use can give a detailed overview of where energy is used and where it can be saved.

DIY Audits: Basic energy assessment tools and checklists are available for those who wish to conduct preliminary audits themselves.

Monitoring Equipment and Systems:

Equipments such as energy meters and monitoring systems can offer real-time feedback on energy use, enabling you to pinpoint energy-intensive processes.

BUILDING AND INFRASTRUCTURE OPTIMIZATION

Insulation and Weatherproofing:

Proper insulation in farm buildings reduces the need for heating and cooling, thereby saving energy. This includes walls, roofs, and especially doors and windows. Weatherstripping and sealing gaps can prevent drafts and energy loss.

Passive Solar Design:

By strategically placing windows, walls, and floors to collect, store, and distribute solar energy in the form of heat, one can reduce the need for artificial heating.

Efficient Lighting:

LEDs: These use up to 75% less energy than traditional incandescent bulbs and last significantly longer.

Natural Lighting: Skylights and strategically placed windows can reduce the need for artificial lighting during the day.

Heating, Ventilation, and Air Conditioning (HVAC):

Regular maintenance and timely upgrades can keep HVAC systems running at peak efficiency.

Installing programmable thermostats can reduce energy consumption by adjusting temperatures according to your needs.

EQUIPMENT AND MACHINERY EFFICIENCY

Regular Maintenance:

Keeping machinery well-maintained ensures they run at optimal efficiency. This includes cleaning, oiling, and timely replacements of worn-out parts.

Upgrading Older Equipment:

Sometimes, the energy savings achieved by using more modern equipment can justify the cost of an upgrade.

Optimal Operation:

Running equipment only when necessary and at the recommended settings can significantly reduce energy consumption.

WATER CONSERVATION AND EFFICIENCY

Efficient Irrigation Systems:

Drip Irrigation: Delivers water directly to plant roots, reducing evaporation and runoff.

Soil Moisture Sensors: These can ensure irrigation only when necessary, based on real-time moisture levels.

Rainwater Harvesting:

Collecting and storing rainwater for future use can reduce the energy costs associated with water pumping.

Recycling and Reusing Water:

With proper filtering and treatment, certain farm operations can recycle water, thereby reducing the total water (and energy) needed.

RENEWABLE ENERGY INTEGRATION

Grid-tied vs. Off-grid:

While going entirely off-grid is ambitious, even grid-tied renewable systems can significantly offset energy costs. The excess energy can sometimes be sold back to the grid.

Battery Storage:

Modern battery storage solutions allow farms to store excess energy for use during non-production periods, further reducing reliance on the grid.

SUSTAINABLE FARMING PRACTICES

No-till or Reduced Tillage:

This not only conserves soil health but also reduces the energy-intensive process of plowing.

Cover Crops:

They can improve soil health and reduce the need for energy-intensive fertilizers.

Integrated Pest Management (IPM):

By reducing the reliance on chemical pesticides, IPM can cut down on the energy used in their production and application.

EDUCATE AND ENGAGE: THE HUMAN FACTOR

Training and Workshops:

Regularly training staff and workers about the importance of energy conservation ensures that everyone is on the same page and practices energy-saving techniques.

Engagement:

Encouraging feedback and suggestions can lead to innovative energy-saving ideas from those who work closely with the farm's operations.

FINANCIAL INCENTIVES AND SUPPORT

Grants and Subsidies:

Many governments and organizations offer financial incentives for energy conservation measures, from upgrading equipment to insulating buildings.

Tax Breaks:

Energy-efficient equipment or practices might qualify for tax deductions or credits, further offsetting their costs.

In the journey towards energy self-sufficiency, every joule saved is as good as one produced. By combining energy conservation with renewable energy production, modern farms can create a resilient, efficient, and truly sustainable operation. The path to energy self-sufficiency is not just about adding new systems but refining and optimizing what's already in place. It's a holistic approach, where every action, no matter how small, contributes to the larger goal of a sustainable, energy-efficient farm.

CHAPTER 8

ECONOMICS OF MINI FARMING

ANALYSIS OF THE COSTS AND BENEFITS OF SELF-SUFFICIENCY

UNDERSTANDING THE FRAMEWORK OF MINI FARMING ECONOMICS

The Concept of Scale: Scaling is fundamental in agriculture. Large commercial farms benefit from economies of scale. In contrast, mini farms operate on a smaller scale, where the dynamics are inherently different. A thorough understanding of these dynamics is crucial for a mini farm's profitability.

Capital Costs vs. Operating Costs: It's essential to differentiate between initial investment (capital costs) and the recurring expenses associated with running a farm (operating costs). A clear division can help in financial planning and break-even analysis.

THE INITIAL INVESTMENT: BREAKING DOWN CAPITAL COSTS

Land Acquisition and Preparation:

Purchasing vs. Leasing: The decision to buy or lease land has significant financial implications. While purchasing involves a large upfront cost, leasing can turn into a recurrent expenditure.

Soil Testing and Enhancement: Costs associated with soil testing and necessary amendments to ensure it's fertile.

Infrastructure Development:

Buildings and Sheds: Cost of erecting barns, storage sheds, greenhouses, and other essential structures.

Irrigation Systems: Initial setup costs for drip irrigation, sprinklers, and other irrigation infrastructure.

Fencing and Security: Essential for protecting the farm against pests and potential intruders.

Equipment and Machinery: The initial cost of acquiring essential machinery, tools, and equipment. This might include tractors, tillers, seeders, and other specialized equipment.

Seed and Livestock Acquisition:

Seed Selection: Costs associated with purchasing high-quality seeds or saplings.

Livestock Purchase: Initial costs of buying animals, be it poultry, cattle, or smaller animals like rabbits.

RECURRING EXPENDITURE: UNPACKING OPERATING COSTS

Seeds and Inputs: The annual or seasonal costs of seeds, fertilizers, and other inputs necessary for crop production.

Livestock Maintenance:

Feed and Nutrition: The recurring costs of purchasing or producing feed.

Healthcare: Expenses associated with vaccinations, treatments, and general animal health maintenance.

Labor: Depending on the scale and intensity of farming operations, labor can be a significant cost, be it hired help or the opportunity cost of the owner's time.

Utilities: Regular expenses like water, electricity, and other utilities, crucial for the smooth operation of the farm.

Repairs and Maintenance: The periodic costs of maintaining machinery, equipment, and infrastructure in good working condition.

REVENUE STREAMS IN MINI FARMING

Crop Sales: Revenue generated from the sale of fruits, vegetables, grains, and other crops.

Livestock Products: This encompasses a wide range of products including, but not limited to, milk, eggs, meat, wool, and honey.

Value-added Products: By processing primary products, one can create jams, cheeses, pickles, and other goods that can fetch a higher price.

Agri-tourism and Workshops: Many modern mini farms diversify their income by inviting tourists or conducting workshops and training sessions.

The Intangible Benefits of Self-sufficiency

Food Security: The assurance of having a continuous supply of fresh and healthy produce, irrespective of external market dynamics.

Health and Nutrition: Growing one's food often means reduced exposure to pesticides, preservatives, and other chemicals commonly found in commercially produced items.

Environmental Benefits: A sustainable mini farm contributes positively to the environment by promoting biodiversity, reducing carbon footprint, and fostering a balanced ecosystem.

Psychological Well-being: There's a profound satisfaction in nurturing plants and animals. The act of farming can be therapeutic and offers a sense of purpose.

NAVIGATING THE ECONOMIC CHALLENGES

Market Dynamics: Understanding the local market, demand fluctuations, and pricing is crucial to ensure profitability.

Risk Management: Diversifying crops, having insurance, and maintaining an emergency fund can help mitigate the risks associated with farming.

Keeping Abreast with Technology: Embracing modern farming techniques and technologies can lead to better yields and reduced costs.

COST-SAVING STRATEGIES IN MINI FARMING

Intercropping and Polyculture: Growing complementary crops together can lead to better land utilization and reduced pest-related issues.

Organic and Natural Farming: By reducing dependence on commercial fertilizers and pesticides, one can significantly bring down input costs.

Community Engagement: Forming or joining cooperatives, community-supported agriculture (CSA) programs, or barter systems can lead to shared resources, reduced costs, and better market access.

EVALUATING ROI (RETURN ON INVESTMENT)

Financial Metrics: Tools like payback period, net present value, and internal rate of return can provide quantitative measures of a farm's profitability.

Beyond Numbers: While quantitative metrics are crucial, the qualitative benefits—food security, health, environmental impact—also play a role in the overall evaluation of a mini farm's success.

In the realm of mini farming, the journey towards self-sufficiency is as much about passion as it is about profits. While the economic aspects are undeniably crucial, the holistic benefits of a balanced ecosystem, food security, and a sense of fulfillment often make the venture truly worthwhile. As with any business, constant learning, adaptation, and a keen understanding of both costs and revenue streams are the keys to success in mini farming.

SELLING PRODUCTS: LOCAL MARKETS, COOPERATION, AND ONLINE

THE IMPORTANCE OF MARKET ACCESS FOR MINI FARMERS

Market Dynamics: Understanding the intricacies of the market is essential. Supply and demand, seasonality, and consumer preferences dictate product viability and pricing.

Revenue Streams: The end goal for most mini farmers is to generate income. Accessing the right markets ensures consistent revenue streams and business sustainability.

Building Brand Reputation: Continued access to, and a positive image in the market, elevates the brand and can garner premium pricing.

LOCAL MARKETS: BRIDGING THE GAP BETWEEN FARM AND CONSUMER

Farmers' Markets:

  Pros: Direct access to consumers, immediate feedback, building relationships, and setting prices.

  Cons: Stall costs, competition, and dependence on market timings and seasonal fluctuations.

Local Grocery Stores and Retail Outlets:

  Pros: Regular orders, wide consumer reach, and consistent revenue.

Cons: Possible lower pricing due to bulk buying, adherence to store's quality standards, and dependence on store's payment cycles.

Direct Sales from Farm:

Pros: Eliminates middlemen, offers an authentic farm experience to buyers, and builds direct relationships.

Cons: Needs on-farm infrastructure, limits audience to locals, and demands regular farm upkeep for visitors.

COOPERATIVES: STRENGTH IN NUMBERS

The Concept of Cooperatives: Agricultural cooperatives are organizations formed by farmers to collectively market their produce, purchase inputs, and sometimes process their products.

Benefits of Joining a Cooperative:

Economies of Scale: Bulk purchasing of inputs can lead to cost savings.

Negotiating Power: Collective selling often results in better price negotiations.

Shared Resources: Shared storage, transportation, and processing facilities reduce individual costs.

Knowledge Sharing: Farmers share best practices, innovations, and solutions to common challenges.

Considerations Before Joining:

Membership Costs: Some cooperatives have joining fees or annual membership costs.

Adherence to Standards: Cooperatives may have strict quality standards that members must adhere to.

Profit Sharing: Profits are typically shared among members, which might differ from individual selling.

DIGITAL PLATFORMS: HARNESSING THE POWER OF THE INTERNET

E-commerce Platforms: Several platforms allow farmers to list their products online, reaching a wider audience.

Pros: Access to a global market, direct communication with buyers, and digital payment methods.

Cons: Listing fees, competition, and potential logistical challenges of shipping.

Social Media Marketing: Using platforms like Instagram, Facebook, and Twitter to market products and tell the farm's story.

> **Pros:** Direct engagement with consumers, ability to use visuals and stories, and relatively low marketing costs.

> **Cons:** Time-consuming, needs consistent content creation, and might require digital marketing skills.

Subscription Models: Offering subscription boxes or Community Supported Agriculture (CSA) memberships where consumers receive regular deliveries.

> **Pros:** Predictable income, fosters loyalty, and reduced marketing costs.

> **Cons:** Commitment to regular deliveries, maintaining product variety, and managing subscriptions.

STRATEGIES FOR PRICING AND PROFITABILITY

Cost-based Pricing: Pricing products based on the total cost of production plus a margin. Ensures that all costs are covered and a profit is made.

Value-based Pricing: Pricing based on the perceived value of the product in the market. This could be higher or lower than cost-based pricing, depending on the product's unique selling proposition.

Competitive Pricing: Setting prices based on what competitors are charging. Essential to understand the local or online market dynamics.

Dynamic Pricing: Adjusting prices based on demand and supply. This strategy often requires a keen understanding of market trends and flexibility.

BUILDING TRUST AND AUTHENTICITY: THE MODERN CONSUMER

Transparency in Practices: The modern consumer values transparency. Sharing farming practices, inputs used, and even challenges faced can foster trust.

Certifications and Labels: Organic, Non-GMO, Fair Trade, etc., can offer an edge in the market but come with their own set of standards and regulations.

Engaging with the Community: Workshops, farm tours, and community events can go a long way in building relationships and loyalty.

DIVERSIFYING SALES CHANNELS: THE KEY TO RESILIENCE

Diversifying sales channels ensures that the farm's income doesn't rely heavily on a single market. This spread of revenue sources can act as a safety net in case one channel faces challenges.

FUTURE TRENDS IN MINI FARMING MARKETING

Sustainable and Eco-friendly Packaging: With a growing emphasis on sustainability, using biodegradable or reusable packaging can be a significant market differentiator.

Blockchain in Agriculture: Blockchain can provide transparency from farm to table, ensuring product authenticity and building trust.

Direct-to-Consumer Tech Platforms: The rise of farm-to-table platforms, apps, and technologies that directly connect farmers with consumers will redefine the traditional market setup.

Navigating the world of selling can be daunting for a mini farmer. Yet, with the right strategies, knowledge of market dynamics, and a bit of innovation, a mini farm's products can find their rightful place in the market, ensuring profitability and sustainability. Whether it's the local farmers' market, a cooperative, or the vast online world, opportunities abound for those willing to explore, learn, and adapt.

SELLING YOUR PRODUCTS

UNDERSTANDING PRODUCT DIFFERENTIATION IN MINI FARMING

Unique Value Proposition (UVP): The UVP is the primary reason your product stands out in the marketplace. For mini farms, this could be the freshness of produce, organic certification, or rare heirloom varieties. Establishing a strong UVP can justify premium pricing.

Branding and Packaging: Having visually appealing and sustainable packaging can influence consumer purchasing decisions. A recognizable logo, a consistent color palette, and a cohesive brand message can establish trust and brand loyalty.

Storytelling: People love to know the origins of their food. Sharing the farm's history, your farming practices, and stories can add a personal touch, making consumers more likely to support your farm.

PRICING STRATEGY: BALANCING COST, COMPETITION, AND CUSTOMER

Cost-Plus Pricing: Determining the total production cost per unit and adding a desired profit margin. This method ensures you cover costs and achieve a consistent profitability level.

Competitive Analysis: Studying how similar products are priced in the market can provide a benchmark. It's essential to consider the perceived value, quality, and brand positioning of competitors.

Skimming and Penetration Pricing: These are strategies to introduce new products. Skimming involves setting high prices for new products to maximize revenue from early adopters, while penetration pricing aims to attract a large customer base by setting lower initial prices.

Dynamic and Seasonal Pricing: Adapting prices based on external factors such as seasonal demand, perishability, or market trends.

UTILIZING DIRECT-TO-CONSUMER CHANNELS

Farm Stands and On-Farm Stores: Setting up a sales point on the farm can reduce middlemen and ensure 100% profit. However, infrastructure and consistent farm upkeep are vital.

Subscription Services: Offering boxes of seasonal produce or products delivered at regular intervals. It can ensure predictable income and help in inventory management.

Online Platforms: Having an e-commerce website or leveraging platforms like Etsy for value-added products can expand your market reach.

WHOLESALE AND RETAIL CONSIDERATIONS

B2B Selling: Selling directly to businesses, such as local restaurants, cafes, or grocery stores, can lead to bulk orders. Establishing a relationship and ensuring consistent quality is crucial.

Contract Farming: Entering into contracts with businesses where you provide specific crops in agreed quantities at predetermined prices. This provides income stability but can be restrictive.

Joining Food Hubs: A food hub is a centrally located facility that facilitates the business management aspects of aggregating, storing, processing, distributing, and selling local and regional food products.

NAVIGATING LOCAL FARMERS' MARKETS

Stall Design and Layout: An attractive stall can draw more customers. Consider factors like signage, product display, and accessibility.

Sampling and Demonstrations: Offering samples or demonstrations can attract attention and stimulate sales.

Building Repeat Customers: Loyalty programs, newsletters, or discount cards can encourage repeat purchases.

Networking: Engaging with other farmers and vendors can open doors for collaboration, shared resources, or bulk purchasing discounts.

VALUE-ADDED PRODUCTS AS AN ADDITIONAL REVENUE STREAM

Types of Value-added Products: Jams, jellies, pickles, dried fruits, sauces, and flavored oils, among others.

Licensing and Regulations: Understand local regulations regarding the production and sale of processed foods.

Pricing and Marketing: Value-added products can often command a higher price. Positioning them as artisanal, handcrafted, or unique can add to their appeal.

COLLABORATIONS AND PARTNERSHIPS

Partnering with Local Businesses: Joint ventures with local restaurants, cafes, or hotels where they exclusively use and promote your products.

Workshops and Classes: Collaborating with local chefs, artisans, or experts to host classes or workshops on the farm.

Pop-Up Events: Hosting or partnering for short-term sales events in urban settings or during local festivals.

LEVERAGING TECHNOLOGY FOR SALES AND MARKETING

Digital Marketing: Utilizing social media platforms, email marketing, and search engine optimization (SEO) to promote products and engage with customers.

Inventory Management Systems: Tools and software that help track products, sales, and inventory levels, ensuring efficient operations.

Mobile Payment Solutions: Providing flexibility in payment methods can enhance customer experience and increase sales.

FEEDBACK MECHANISM AND CONTINUOUS IMPROVEMENT

Customer Feedback: Actively seeking feedback can help understand consumer preferences, quality concerns, or areas of improvement.

Regular Market Analysis: Staying updated with market trends, competitor activities, and changing consumer behavior is essential to adapt and grow.

Continuous Learning: Attending workshops, webinars, or courses can introduce new techniques, tools, or strategies.

In the realm of mini farming, every product carries the stamp of hard work, dedication, and love for the land. Successfully selling these products is not just about revenue; it's about sharing the fruits of labor with the community and celebrating the virtues of sustainable agriculture. By effectively positioning, pricing, and promoting products, a mini farm can thrive in today's competitive marketplace, making the journey from farm to fork both profitable and fulfilling.

STRATEGIES FOR A SUSTAINABLE RETURN ON INVESTMENT

THE FINANCIAL FRAMEWORK OF MINI FARMING

Initial Capital Investment: Evaluate the necessary start-up costs, including land acquisition, infrastructure setup, equipment purchase, and seed capital.

Operational Costs: Regular expenses such as seeds, fertilizers, pest control, labor, water, electricity, and marketing efforts fall under this category. A clear understanding of monthly and seasonal expenditures is crucial.

Revenue Streams: Apart from primary product sales, identify other potential sources of income, like agritourism, workshops, or value-added products.

Breakeven Analysis: Calculate the point at which the farm's revenues will cover all incurred costs. This is crucial to gauge the sustainability and viability of the venture.

DIVERSIFYING FARM PRODUCTION

Polyculture Farming: By growing multiple crops together, farmers can ensure that they don't rely on a single product. This approach reduces economic risks linked to crop failure or market price fluctuations.

Livestock Integration: Incorporating small-scale livestock rearing can provide additional revenue from meat, eggs, or dairy. Livestock also contribute to farm sustainability by providing manure and assisting in pest control.

Value-added Products: Transforming primary products into something of higher value, such as making jams, sauces, or cheeses, can significantly boost revenues.

EFFICIENT RESOURCE MANAGEMENT

Water Conservation: Implement techniques like drip irrigation, rainwater harvesting, and mulching to reduce water costs.

Integrated Pest Management (IPM): Using beneficial insects, companion planting, and organic repellents can significantly reduce expenses on chemical pesticides.

Recycling and Composting: Converting farm waste into compost not only reduces the need for external fertilizers but also enhances soil health.

INVESTING IN TECHNOLOGY

Automation: Equipments like automatic seed planters, irrigation systems, or chicken feeders can reduce labor costs.

Digital Platforms: Invest in a user-friendly website and e-commerce platforms to reach a wider audience without the constraints of physical location.

Precision Farming: Utilize tools and software for soil analysis, weather predictions, and market trend analysis to make informed farming decisions.

CONTINUOUS LEARNING AND SKILL DEVELOPMENT

Workshops and Training: Stay updated with the latest farming techniques, market trends, and business strategies by attending relevant workshops or online courses.

Networking: Joining farmer associations or co-operatives can provide opportunities to share resources, insights, and collectively negotiate better deals with suppliers or buyers.

EFFICIENT MARKETING AND BRANDING

Target Market Identification: Understand the demographics, preferences, and buying habits of your target audience.

Unique Selling Proposition (USP): Position the products in a way that stands out in the market, such as organic, heirloom, or locally-sourced.

Digital Presence: Leverage social media marketing, content creation, and online advertisements to reach and engage with a broader audience.

EXPANSION AND SCALING

Reinvesting Profits: Allocate a portion of the profits back into the farm to improve infrastructure, diversify offerings, or enhance marketing efforts.

Crowdfunding and Grants: For significant expansion projects, consider crowdfunding platforms or look for agricultural grants offered by governmental bodies.

Partnership and Collaborations: Joint ventures or collaborations with restaurants, cafes, or other businesses can offer stable contracts and bulk orders.

RISK MANAGEMENT AND CONTINGENCY PLANNING

Crop Insurance: Insuring the crops can safeguard against potential losses due to unforeseen natural calamities or diseases.

Diversified Investment: Avoid putting all financial resources into one aspect of the farm. Spread out investments to reduce risks.

Emergency Funds: Maintain a reserve of funds to handle unexpected expenses or downturns, ensuring the farm's continuity during challenging times.

EVALUATING AND ADJUSTING STRATEGIES

Regular Financial Audits: Conduct detailed financial reviews to understand profitability, cost centers, and areas of improvement.

Feedback Mechanism: Encourage customer feedback to understand market needs and adjust products or services accordingly.

Market Trend Analysis: Keep an eye on market shifts, consumer preferences, and technological advancements to adapt and evolve.

In the domain of mini farming, achieving a sustainable return on investment is not solely about maximizing profits. It intertwines economic viability with environmental responsibility and community engagement. By integrating efficient farming practices, diversifying income streams, leveraging technology, and staying adaptable to changing market dynamics, modern farm owners can ensure their mini farms not only thrive but also contribute positively to the larger ecosystem.

CONCLUSION

Throughout our comprehensive exploration of mini farming, we've meticulously unraveled its intricacies, spanning techniques, challenges, and the undeniable potential it holds for urban and suburban spaces. Mini farming stands as a testament to the marriage of age-old agricultural wisdom and today's innovative approaches, offering solutions that are both strategic and adaptable to the constraints of limited spaces.

As we gaze into the horizon, it's clear that the significance of mini farming will only burgeon. With escalating urbanization and the increasing premium on land, this compact approach to agriculture champions local food production and could significantly reduce the vast expanses traditionally dedicated to farming. As technology continues to evolve, smart irrigation, AI-driven monitoring, and other innovations will no doubt find their place within mini farming, propelling it to new heights of efficiency and productivity.

But beyond the tangible benefits in terms of yield and space optimization, mini farming heralds profound implications for our health, environment, and societal fabric. By pivoting towards this model, we inch closer to a world with enhanced access to fresh, chemical-free produce, thereby promoting healthier dietary choices. From an ecological vantage point, it signifies a stride towards sustainable farming, curtailing the environmental impacts associated with extensive land use and long-distance food transportation. On a communal level, mini farms can act as cohesive hubs, weaving together communities in shared endeavors and fostering a sense of collective purpose.

In its essence, mini farming transcends being a mere agricultural methodology. It encapsulates a vision of a sustainable, health-conscious, and community-driven future. As stewards of the modern farming realm, we find ourselves at the nexus of this transformative journey, holding the potential to reshape the contours of contemporary agriculture.

Printed in Great Britain
by Amazon

34144364R00110